National Park Service
U.S. Department of the Interior

Fire Island National Seashore
Patchogue, New York

Fire Island National Seashore:
Alternative Transportation Study

PMIS No. 125892A/17089
December 2011

John A. Volpe National Transportation Systems Center
Research and Innovative Technology Administration
U.S. Department of Transportation

Table of Contents

Acknowledgements 4
Section 1: Introduction 1
Section 2: Planning and Development Context 9
Section 3: Transportation Overview 20
Section 4: Water-based Transport 28
Section 5: Vehicular Use Patterns 42
Section 6: Conclusions 57
Appendix A: Stakeholder Table 69
Appendix B: NPS Driving Dates & Times 71
Appendix C: Fire Island School District Bus Routes 73

Figures, Tables, and Images

Figure 1: Fire Island National Seashore and Communities 2
Figure 2: Fire Island National Seashore Regional Context 7
Figure 3: Jurisdiction Map 20
Figure 4: Transportation Networks: Robert Moses S.P. to Atlantique 20
Figure 5: Transportation Networks: Robbins Rest to Sailors Haven 21
Figure 6: Transportation Networks: Cherry Grove to Watch Hill 22
Figure 7: Docks West: Lighthouse to Sailors Haven 34
Figure 8: Docks East: Cherry Grove to Bellport Beach 35
Figure 9: Schematic Map of User Groups 39
Figure 10: Seasonality and Intensity of Vehicular Use 40
Table 1: Community Structures 24
Table 2: Dock and Ferry Table 57
Image 1: Ferry Departing Ocean Bay Park 14
Image 2: Propane Delivery at Fire Island Pines 32

Acknowledgements

Diane Abell
Landscape Architect / Park Planner, Fire Island National Seashore

Ellen Carlson
Community Planner, National Park Service – Northeast Region

Jay Lippert
Chief Ranger, Fire Island National Seashore

John Mahoney
Division of Resource and Visitor Protection, Fire Island National Seashore

Christopher Soller
Superintendent, Fire Island National Seashore

Additional key contacts and interviewed stakeholders are included in the Stakeholder Table in Appendix A.

Section 1: Introduction

Project Overview

As part of its General Management Plan (GMP) process, Fire Island National Seashore (FIIS) seeks to develop a long-term management model to protect Fire Island's resources, while facilitating a safe, rewarding, and relevant experience for the public. The new General Management Plan will update and replace the existing GMP, written in 1977. As part of this management model, the Seashore is seeking the best and most appropriate methods for moving people, goods, and services to, from, and along Fire Island. The transportation challenge addressed by this report is to balance the many kinds of vehicle use on the Island with the Seashore's resource protection mission and the desire of residents and visitors to preserve the Island's "roadless" nature.

The GMP analysis consists of four planning alternatives: (1) No Action/Status Quo/ Current Management, (2) Enhancing Natural Resource Values, (3) Recognizing the Relationship between Humans and Nature, and (4) Explore New Opportunities for Public Use. The latter three alternatives represent a spectrum between actively managing the Seashore with an emphasis on resource protection to developing and managing the Seashore with an emphasis on public use. While the preferred alternative has not yet been formally selected, FIIS has directed that this transportation analysis be conducted using Alternative 3, which emphasizes a balance between public use and resource protection. The goals and approach of Alternative 3 form the context for the analysis of existing conditions, needs, and challenges. It is anticipated that transportation alternatives selected will have relevance to each of the four GMP alternatives.

This report first describes the existing conditions on Fire Island with respect to transportation infrastructure, usage, and constraints. It organizes and clarifies the complex transportation systems on Fire Island, including an assessment of the key needs and challenges of various stakeholder groups. In particular, it describes vehicle use in the most detail possible. The characterization of existing conditions will provide a basis from which to identify and evaluate alternative transportation opportunities for the future, with the aim of encouraging more water-based access to Fire Island, wherever practical, as a substitute for vehicle use.

These opportunities represent only a starting point for further consideration, because the specific issues of vehicle use have previously been no better defined than the vehicle use itself. Neither the Seashore nor stakeholders interviewed by project staff identified particular types of vehicles or dates and times of driving as problematic, or whether particular effects of vehicle use (e.g., safety, congestion, noise, pollution, aesthetics) were contributing factors. There is some indication as to the nature of the issues in the "Ethnographic Overview and Assessment" conducted in 2004:

> "Many communities experience some tension among seasonal residents, year-round residents, the Park Service, and—if present—business interests. Year-round residents see themselves, correctly, as the ones who keep the island going....and say they are tolerant of the seasonal population, even welcoming, [while] feeling that the seasonals "don't want us here". This sentiment appears mostly with regard to driving vehicles along the interior walks, in most cases for necessary functions such as collecting garbage. The year-rounders do the driving and it upsets seasonal residents who cherish the traffic-free quality of island life."[1]

This offers an indication as to the particulars of a "driving problem". A 2008 visitor study and annual visitor surveys also document concerns about the amount of driving on Fire Island. As a result, the opportunities include proposals for better characterizing these aspects of the problem.

---

[1] 2005. Ethnographic Overview and Assessment. National Park Service, 100.

Fire Island Description

Fire Island is a narrow barrier island, 32 miles in length, located off the south coast of Long Island in Suffolk County, New York. The island includes authorized areas of the National Seashore, Robert Moses State Park, Smith Point County Park, and private land, including 17 distinct communities. Saltaire and Ocean Beach are the only two of the 17 communities that are incorporated villages. The island lies within the Towns of Babylon, Islip, and Brookhaven, though all Federally-owned lands lie within Islip and Brookhaven (see Figure 1). The communities have a combined seasonal resident population of between 12,000 and 16,000 as well as approximately 500 year-round residents.

Fire Island National Seashore is a National Park Service (NPS) unit consisting of ocean beaches, dunes, maritime forests on Fire Island, and parts of the Great South Bay and Moriches Bay, as well as the William Floyd Estate on Long Island. NPS maintains jurisdiction over resource management for the 26 linear miles of the Island within the NPS boundary and parts of the surrounding waterways, although lands owned by other public and private entities are governed independently while subject to certain NPS regulations. NPS has governing jurisdiction over beaches, NPS sites, the Otis Pike Fire Island High Dunes Wilderness, other Federally-owned lands, and waterways within the authorized boundary. Smith Point County Park and all 17 communities are within the NPS boundary.

Fire Island is located approximately 40 miles east of New York City and approximately 60 miles west of the eastern tip of Long Island. Fire Island is located east of Jones Beach, a heavily-visited barrier-island beach destination for New York City and Long Island residents. Robert Moses State Park is located on the western end of Fire Island and includes facilities for beach recreation, fishing, boating, and golf. Smith Point County Park is located within the boundary of the Park, immediately east of the Federal wilderness area and contains facilities for beach recreation, camping, and off-road vehicle recreation. Bridges connecting Fire Island to Long Island enable vehicular access to the western and easternmost ends of the Park.

Figure 1
Fire Island National Seashore and Communities
Source: Volpe Center

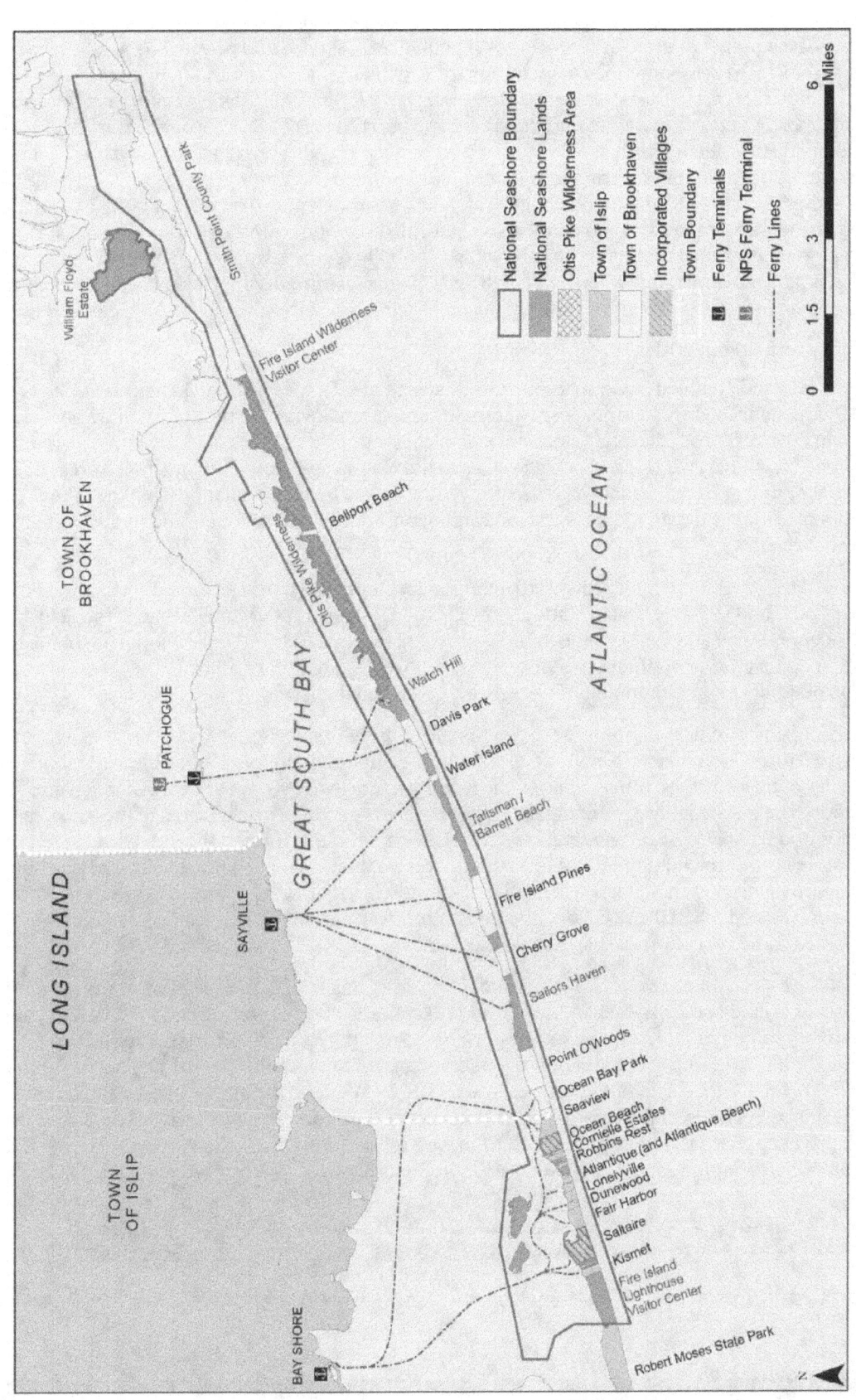

With its mosaic of ownership and governance and its "roadless" infrastructure built primarily to accommodate pedestrian traffic, Fire Island has a unique and complex transportation system that is largely independent of conventional vehicular access. Most people and goods travel to the Island by water-based transportation, in the form of scheduled ferry service and private boats. NPS also permits up to 418 vehicles to drive onto the Island during the driving season, which generally runs from the Tuesday after Columbus Day to the week before Memorial Day (also includes some weekdays in June and September). Vehicles can access the Island via the Robert Moses Causeway on the west end, crossing into FIIS jurisdiction about one-half mile west of the Fire Island Lighthouse gate, or via the William Floyd Parkway on the east end, crossing through the checkpoint at the Wilderness Visitor Center and driving along the beach for 6.8 miles to reach the Watch Hill Visitor Center. The vast majority of vehicles enter from the west. Some visitors and employees enter FIIS by foot or by bicycle, after parking at Robert Moses State Park or at Smith Point County Park. Mobility on the Island is also highly dependent upon tides, piping plover season (when parts of the beach are closed to driving), and visitation levels (seasonal congestion on main thoroughfares by people on foot inhibits safe movement of vehicles and bicycles).

History and Communities

The Fire Island National Seashore came into existence in 1964 when Congress passed Public Law 88-587. FIIS was established "for the purpose of conserving and preserving for the use of future generations certain relatively unspoiled and undeveloped beaches, dunes, and other natural features within Suffolk County, New York, which possess high values to the Nation as examples of unspoiled areas of great natural beauty in close proximity to large concentrations of urban population."[2] At the time of the National Seashore designation, Fire Island was the only developed barrier island in the United States without roads.

Many of the communities and early settlements, which initially were established around the Fire Island Lighthouse and U.S. Life Saving Stations, expanded in the resort era, which began in the 1870s as abundant hunting and fishing opportunities attracted tourists. Real estate development, in the form of summer bungalows, had flourished since the early 1920s and became prolific in the 1950s. By 1964, about 2,500 buildings and 17 communities were firmly rooted on the Island.[3]

A key impetus to citizen support for the National Seashore designation was the threat of a roadway. Robert Moses, a prominent New York City and State public employee responsible for building hundreds of miles of highways and other major public infrastructure in the New York metropolitan area, first proposed an ocean parkway running the length of Fire Island in 1930, and again in the 1950s, raising fierce opposition from Fire Island seasonal residents. In 1962, residents formed the Fire Island Association to advocate against the fulfillment of Moses' plan. Around this time, the National Park Service was in the process of acquiring coastal lands for national seashores, as part of an effort to expand the park system to eastern lands. Much of the residents' support for the designation of Fire Island as a national seashore stemmed from their efforts to block the ocean parkway.

Fire Island's 17 communities are distinct and diverse, ranging from quiet vacation towns to communities with year-round residents, including families with children and supporting commercial and public services. The communities follow similar development patterns: a commercial center, if one exists, is along the bay side; one or more lateral streets transect the community; and parallel north-south narrow walks are lined with single-family houses on small plots. While communities may be similar in form and appearance, residents emphasize the distinctiveness of each community, which are described in further detail in later sections. The communities, from west to east, are: Kismet, Saltaire, Fair Harbor, Dunewood, Lonelyville, Atlantique and Atlantique Beach,[4] Robbins Rest, Fire Island Summer Club, Cornielle Estates,

---

[2] National Park Service. 1977. Fire Island National Seashore General Management Plan. United States Department of the Interior / National Park Service. Accessed 23 March 2010: http://www.nps.gov/fiis/parkmgmt/1977-general-management-plan.htm., 1.
[3] Ethnographic Overview, 1.
[4] Atlantique Beach is a recreational marina and beach area owned by the Town of Islip and considered part of the Atlantique community.

Ocean Beach, Seaview, Ocean Bay Park, Point O' Woods, Cherry Grove, Fire Island Pines, Water Island, and Davis Park.

Description of NPS Areas

Due to its close proximity to major population centers, including the New York City metropolitan area, FIIS attracts heavy seasonal visitation. The visitor use areas of FIIS include the William Floyd Estate, a 613-acre site containing the historic home and grounds of William Floyd, which is located in Mastic Beach on Long Island. Approximately 4,000 people visit the William Floyd Estate annually. Most visitors come by private car but access is also available via Suffolk County Transit and many local residents walk or bike to the site to take advantage of recreation on the grounds.

With the exception of William Floyd Estate, all visitor use areas are located on Fire Island. Although some facilities on Fire Island are closed during winter, the Park is open year round. The vast majority of visitation occurs during the summer months. Concession services at Sailors Haven and Watch Hill Visitor Centers operate from mid-May through mid-October, due in part to limited ferry service in the off-season.

NPS has use and occupancy rights granted by the State of New York in perpetuity, and along with concurrent jurisdiction, for 26 linear miles of oceanfront beach, from the mean high water line to 1,000 feet into the Atlantic Ocean. Excluding the private communities, NPS has use and occupancy rights for approximately 13.2 oceanside linear beach miles[5] of land on the Island. Visitors can access the lighthouse by foot along the Burma Road from the community of Kismet or from the Field 5 parking lot at Robert Moses State Park. Visitors to Sailors Haven may walk from the communities of Cherry Grove or Point O' Woods, but many take the ferry from Sayville. Visitors to Watch Hill may walk from the community of Davis Park or take the ferry from Patchogue. Finally, visitors to the Wilderness Visitor Center must walk from the parking lot at Smith Point County Park. While NPS does not charge a user's fee for any of its properties on Fire Island, visitors do have to pay for parking at the State and County parks or pay for ferry tickets to access NPS sites and private communities.

Visitation

In addition to the year-round and seasonal residents, approximately 600,000 people visit Fire Island annually. Visitation is calculated by the National Park Service to include the following: visitors entering FIIS Visitor Centers, visitors arriving by ferry at Sailors Haven and Watch Hill, private boats staying at NPS marinas (multiplied by an average boat occupancy), and walk-in visitors through the east and west checkpoints. Visitation has fluctuated between 570,000 and 820,000 between 2000 and 2009.[6] Of the designated NPS visitor use areas, the Fire Island Lighthouse is among the most heavily visited; 41 percent of visitors surveyed in 2008 had visited the lighthouse. Approximately 75,000 visitors in 2009 walked to the Lighthouse from Robert Moses State Park, and others arrive on school buses and other vehicles for field trips and special events. The number of Lighthouse visitors was approximately 125,000 in 2009, according to NPS records.

For purposes of estimating the total number of people on Fire Island during peak visitation periods, a rough estimation of day-use visitors during peak summer weekend days was conducted and found to be approximately 5,850.[7] These visitors are in addition to the 500 year-round residents and 12,000 to 16,000 seasonal residents estimated to be on the Island during the summer season.[8]

---

[5] The entire shoreline within the FIIS boundary, including the bay side and islands in the Great South Bay, is about 65 miles, measured using GIS tools.

[6] NPS Stats. 2010. Fire Island Annual Summary Report for 2009. National Park Service Public Use Statistics Office. Accessed 23 March, 2010: http://www.nature.nps.gov/stats/viewReport.cfm.

[7] Volpe Center staff estimates the day-use visitors based on NPS monthly visitation reports for July 2009 (visitors walking onto Fire Island and arriving by private boat and ferry to NPS sites, total of which was approximately 3,600) and the number of ferry trips departing to Fire Island communities before noon on weekends. Based on conversations with ferry operators, the estimate assumes that 75 percent of passengers on Saturday morning ferries in eastern communities are day visitors and 50 percent of passengers in western communities are day visitors, that these boats operate at 50% of their capacity during peak summer weekends, and that a

A visitor survey administered in July 2008 surveyed people at each of the NPS visitor use areas. The survey provides some insights into recent visitation trends for FIIS. The survey found that 84 percent of visitors were from New York State and 88 percent lived within 45 miles of Fire Island, including visitors from Connecticut and New Jersey, with only three percent of visitors from international origins. About one-third of visitors had visited the park five or more times in the past year. Fifty-seven percent spent less than 24 hours in the park, while 43 percent spent more than 24 hours. The average length of stay for all visitors was 1.1 days, but nearly half of visitors (47%) who spent more than 24 hours in the park stayed for 4 or more nights, indicating likelihood that these visitors were staying in homes in the communities.

As visitors cannot drive directly to NPS sites or communities, 100 percent of visitors surveyed traveled first to a gateway destination, either a ferry terminal or a parking lot at Robert Moses State Park or Smith Point County Park. The survey found that 67 percent of visitors used private vehicles to travel to a ferry terminal or a gateway parking lot on Fire Island. The study noted that 28 percent of all Fire Island visitors surveyed used a public ferry service and 27 percent used private boats to get to the Island (visitors could record more than one mode of travel). When surveyed about the last mode of transportation used before park entry, 36 percent traveled by vehicle, 24 percent traveled by private boat, and 21 percent used a public ferry. Nine percent of visitors arrived at a gateway location by Long Island Railroad (LIRR) and then most likely transferred to a ferry to reach Fire Island, though the survey did not record intermodal transfers.

More than half of visitors surveyed at NPS sites did not visit communities or residential areas. Of the 46 percent that did visit the communities, they were most likely to visit Davis Park, Kismet, Ocean Beach, and Cherry Grove.

Attractions

Visitors to Fire Island come primarily to use the beaches, but many also take advantage of additional FIIS attractions on NPS lands and in private communities. The Fire Island Lighthouse is among the most heavily visited, via walking trails from Robert Moses State Park and school buses and other vehicles serving the site for field trips and special events.

The Sailors Haven developed area contains a Visitor center, a marina, a snack bar, restroom/shower facilities, and beach facilities with lifeguards (all facilities open seasonally). Sailors Haven is adjacent to Sunken Forest, a mature maritime forest with a popular nature trail. Visitors may access the site via ferry service from Sayville, and they may also walk along a concrete path connecting Sailors Haven with Cherry Grove (a distance of under a mile).

Watch Hill developed area features a Visitor Center, a marina, a general store, a restaurant and open-air bar, a campground, restroom/shower facilities, and beach facilities with lifeguards (all facilities open seasonally). Visitors access Watch Hill primarily by ferry from Patchogue or by private boat; visitors can also walk from Davis Park.

Barrett Beach/Talisman is one of the least-developed NPS visitation areas. Located near the center of Fire Island (between the communities of Fire Island Pines and Water Island), the facility contains a dock for loadings and unloading only, a boardwalk trail crossing the width of the Island, restrooms, and two picnic areas. Barrett Beach/Talisman is only accessible by private boat and by foot. During the summer season, this area is heavily used by recreational boaters, both day use visitors and overnight visitors who stay in their self-contained private boats.

The Fire Island Wilderness Visitor Center is accessible from Smith Point County Park and features a small interpretive center and office. The Visitor Center also serves as a gateway and checkpoint for persons entering the Otis Pike Fire Island National Wilderness and for vehicles traveling down the beach.

---

reasonable average capacity for these ferries is 300 passengers (the boats range in capacity from approximately 100 passengers to approximately 400 passengers, and it is assumed that the higher capacity boats are used during peak summer weekends). The estimate of ferry passengers to private communities is 2,250.

[8] For more information about resident population estimates, see "Population" in Section 2.

Several of the private communities offer commercial amenities, such as restaurants, bars, and entertainment venues, that serve as destinations for visitors. Key commercial enclaves include Bayview Walk in Cherry Grove, Bay Walk in Ocean Beach, restaurants in Fire Island Pines and Kismet, the marina area in Ocean Bay Park, and Davis Park Casino. Visitors may access these communities by ferry or by walking from nearby communities or from NPS sites.

Regional Transportation Overview

The extensive transportation networks associated with the densely populated areas of New York City and the Long Island suburbs allow for relative ease of access to Fire Island's gateway towns (see Figure 2). Bay Shore, Sayville, and Patchogue are each located along Sunrise Highway, a four-lane arterial roadway approximately two miles south of the Long Island Expressway (I-495). The gateway towns are all served by the Montauk Branch of LIRR. Fire Island is served by three ferry companies offering passenger service to the public as well as several private and barge services. Close coordination between LIRR and ferry schedules allows visitors to access the Island from New York City without the use of a personal vehicle. Suffolk County Transit offers two seasonal bus routes to Robert Moses State Park and Smith Point County Park and two bus routes that access William Floyd Estate. Two vehicle ferries carry passengers and vehicles across the Long Island Sound (from New London, Connecticut, to Orient Point on Long Island, and from Bridgeport, Connecticut, to Port Jefferson on Long Island). Fire Island is also located in close proximity to three commercial airports, including two major international airports (John F. Kennedy International Airport, LaGuardia International Airport, and Long Island Islip MacArthur Airport).

Report Methodology

A team from the Volpe National Transportation Systems Center / U.S. Department of Transportation (Volpe Center) collected information for the Existing Conditions Report through two site visits to Fire Island National Seashore and phone interviews with key stakeholders. The first site visit took place September 16 – 18, 2009, and included tours of all NPS sites and communities on Fire Island and NPS sites on Long Island. This site visit also included meetings with NPS staff and Fire Island Ferries operators. The second site visit focused on stakeholder interviews and took place December 2 – 4, 2009. Volpe Center and NPS staff interviewed 34 individuals in six group meetings, organized by user group, over the three-day period. Volpe Center staff conducted phone interviews with approximately eight to ten additional stakeholders that were unavailable during the second site visit. In addition to the formal interviews, Volpe Center staff collected information for this report from relevant literature, Internet research, and informal telephone research. A complete list of stakeholders who contributed to this report is included in Appendix A.

Figure 2
Fire Island National Seashore Regional Context
Source: Volpe Center

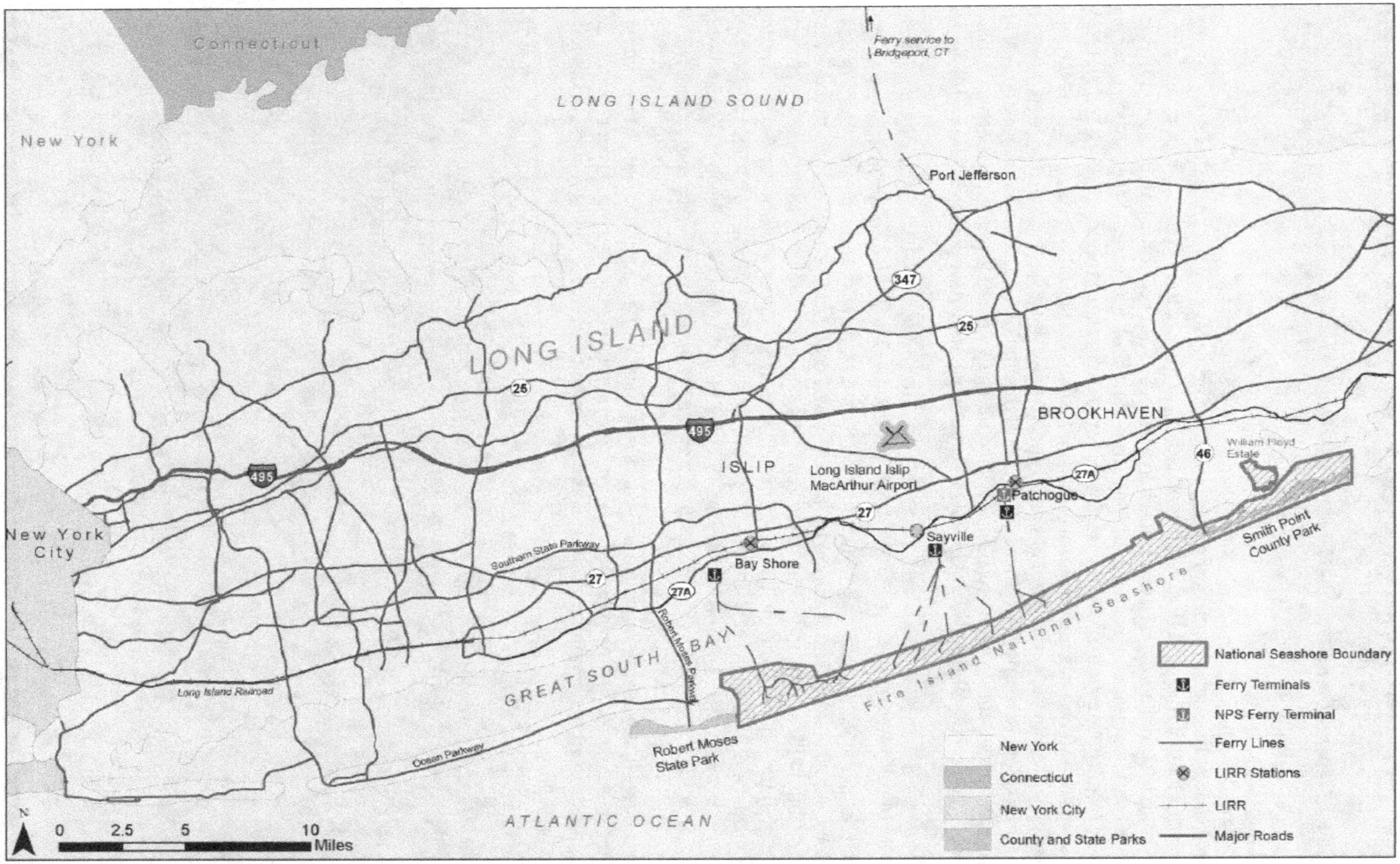

Section 2: Planning and Development Context

Transportation systems on Fire Island have developed in the context of regulations set by various management bodies. Public and private land owners on the Island are subject to a series of rules, ranging from Federal legislation to regulations set by independent villages and restrictions imposed by community associations. The multiple jurisdictions governing Fire Island influence the development and infrastructure patterns, affecting how people and goods move to, from, and within the Island.

Jurisdiction

Fire Island is governed under several tiers of authority. The Island is under the jurisdiction of the National Park Service, the State of New York, and Suffolk County. Sections of the Island are under the jurisdiction of the Towns of Islip and Brookhaven and the Villages of Saltaire and Ocean Beach.

Federal

All of Fire Island, with the exception of Robert Moses State Park and including waterways delineated on Figure 3, is within the jurisdiction of Fire Island National Seashore. NPS rangers enforce federal regulations under the United States Code and the Code of Federal Regulations, Title 36, common to all NPS units. Title 36 contains regulations for zoning standards and regulation of motor vehicle operation, aircraft operation, and personal watercraft operation.

The FIIS Superintendent is responsible for issuing residential and commercial driving permits and has the authority to make and enforce unit-specific regulations to maintain public health and safety, protect natural resources, and achieve other park goals. NPS also has policing authority to enforce hunting and fishing laws, as well as other applicable New York state laws. NPS directly manages all Federally-owned lands (those shown in green on Figure 3) and patrols NPS sites.

County

Fire Island lies within Suffolk County, the largest county on Long Island, extending from the Towns of Huntington and Babylon in the west to Orient Point on the north fork and Montauk on the South Fork. Most of the County's Long Island population is concentrated in its western part, closer to Fire Island, while eastern parts of Suffolk County are rural in character.

Suffolk County is responsible for emergency management and law enforcement on Fire Island, due in part to the County's available resources. The Suffolk County Police Department (SCPD) maintains a regular police patrol on Fire Island for law enforcement and security, except in incorporated villages and on NPS lands. SCPD can enforce state or Federal laws anywhere on Fire Island. SCPD also includes the Suffolk County Marine Bureau, which maintains and mans six police booths (located in Kismet, Atlantique, Ocean Bay Park, Cherry Grove, Fire Island Pines, and Davis Park) and has approximately 11 officers regularly on patrol during the summer season.

Mutual aid arrangements among members of the Fire Island Law Enforcement Safety Council[9] call for the use of Suffolk County resources (such as ambulances and boats) during emergency situations for all parts of Fire Island. Two deputy fire coordinators from the County live on Fire Island and monitor emergency response on the Island, maintaining constant communication with the mainland County units. Suffolk County also coordinates the radio communication systems linking emergency service providers throughout Fire Island and the rest of the County. Emergency services and law enforcement use patterns are described in greater detail in Section 5.

---

[9] The Fire Island Law Enforcement Safety Council consists of the agencies that provide public safety services on Fire Island. Members include the National Park Service, the Suffolk County Police Department, the Town of Islip Office of Emergency Management, the Town of Brookhaven Fire Prevention, the Village of Ocean Beach Police Department, the Village of Saltaire Security, and volunteer fire departments from across the Island.

The Suffolk County Public Works department maintains William Floyd Parkway and the drawbridge to Smith Point County Park, which serve as the only vehicular access route into the eastern end of Fire Island. They also manage the Smith Point County Park and facilities, including the parking lot that serves the eastern reaches of NPS lands near the Fire Island Wilderness Visitor Center. The County is involved with dredging projects, including the dredging of Moriches Inlet on the eastern side of Fire Island and Fire Island Inlet on the west side of the Island, and monitoring of endangered species on Fire Island.

Municipal

Fire Island National Seashore lies within both the Town of Islip and the Town of Brookhaven. The town line separating Islip and Brookhaven passes through the Fire Island community of Seaview. All communities east of Seaview are within the Town of Brookhaven, and all communities west of Seaview are within the Town of Islip. Seaview is split between both towns (see Figure 3). Islip does not maintain jurisdiction over Ocean Beach and Saltaire; both of these incorporated villages establish and enforce their own codes and regulations and maintain their own public facilities. Both towns establish regulatory codes that apply to private lands. Town departments have responsibility for emergency management, road maintenance, public facilities, and public works projects. The towns also permit golf carts and UTVs that operate within the communities (vehicles that stay within community boundaries do not need to be permitted and monitored by NPS). Some communities have homeowners associations that provide additional rules, guidelines, or governing structures.

The Town of Islip manages several facilities and systems on Fire Island, some of which are managed cooperatively with other jurisdictions. The Islip Department of Public Works is responsible for building and maintaining concrete walks for all communities on Fire Island within the town, with the exception of Saltaire and Ocean Beach. The town emergency management and Engineering coordinates with NPS about beach replenishment. The Islip Parks Department builds and maintains all wooden boardwalks within its jurisdiction. The Parks Department maintains the Town park of Atlantique Beach, including a full marina, bathhouse facilities, a concession stand, and accessory buildings. The Department also maintains a park and tennis court in Kismet. The town of Islip Public Safety Enforcement, Code Enforcement, Fire Marshall, and Building Department perform code inspections and enforcement in the beach communities. Islip's departments also respond to code violations and complaints and assist in law enforcement investigations.

The Town of Islip Emergency Management Department serves on the Fire Island Law Enforcement Safety Council and maintains close communications with other law enforcement and emergency services personnel serving the Island. A key responsibility of the Emergency Management Department is evacuation for major storms. They support village, community, and NPS agencies for rescue management, fire, and emergency services, as needed.

The Town of Brookhaven also serves on the Fire Island Law Enforcement Safety Council and works cooperatively with other Safety Council members. The Brookhaven Code Enforcement and Building divisions perform code inspections in beach communities, respond to code violation complaints, and assist in general law enforcement investigations. The Brookhaven Environmental Department has been involved with beach re-nourishment, in cooperation with the Town of Islip and NPS, and the Town manages dock reconstruction and dredging projects in the Brookhaven communities. The Highway Department travels to Fire Island on a daily basis, year-round, to build and repair boardwalks, traveling by both vehicle and barge. Finally, the Town owns and operates the Davis Park marina and Great Gun Marina inside Smith Point County Park, which is open during the summer season to Brookhaven residents and non-residents. The Village of Bellport also maintains a dock at Bellport Beach, which bisects the Otis Pike Fire Island High Dunes Wilderness.

The incorporated villages of Saltaire and Ocean Beach have jurisdiction over their communities, including maintaining and enforcing village codes. The communities also maintain walks and boardwalks, public facilities and buildings, fire and police departments. Saltaire does not have a sworn officer force; the village has certified security guards that do not have arrest powers or ability to carry weapons and relies upon SCPD for police services.

Figure 3
Jurisdiction Map
Source: Volpe Center

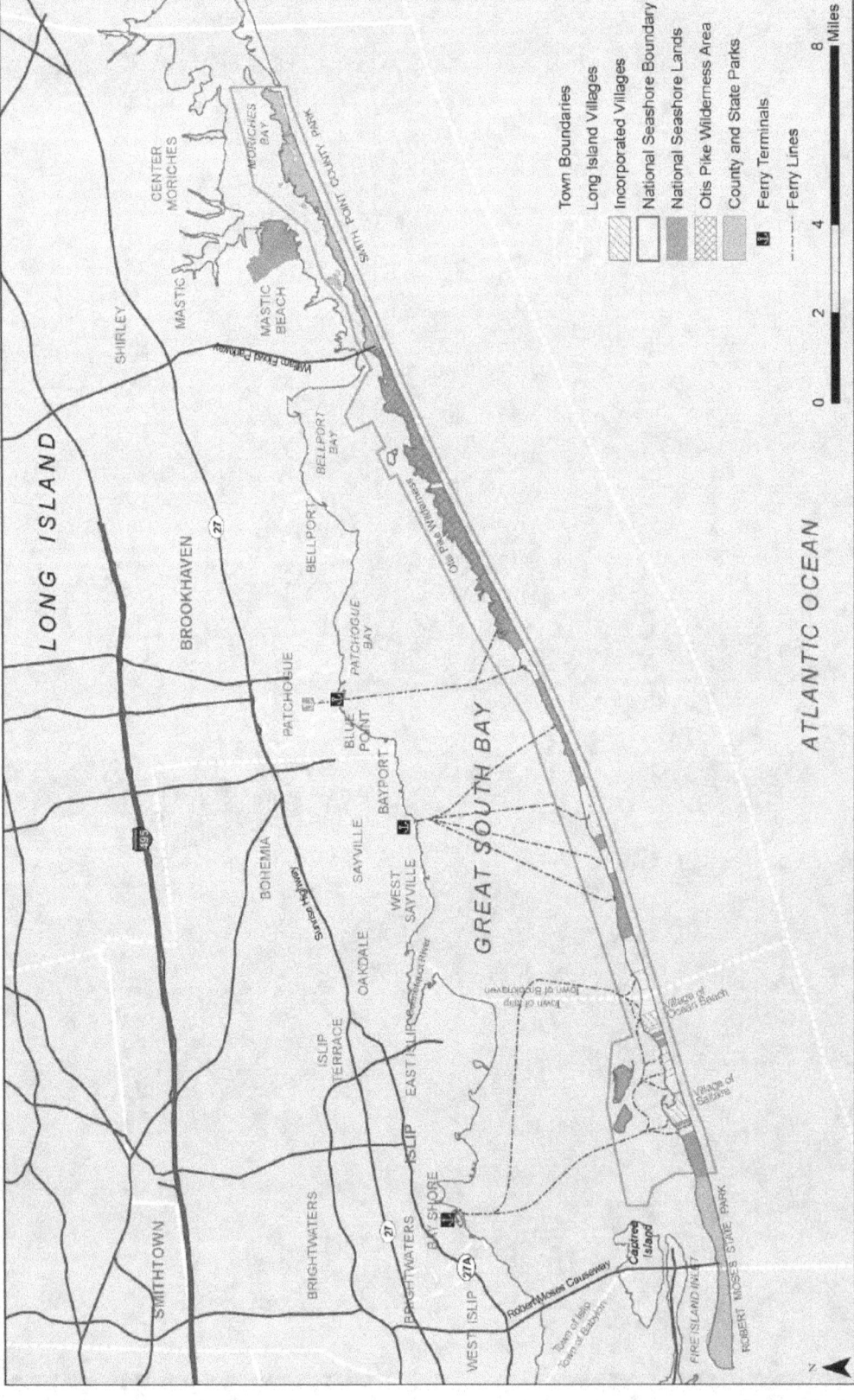

Zoning and Development Codes

The towns and villages establish and enforce regulations pertaining to zoning and development codes, garbage, vehicle usage, harbor management, sewers, tax enforcement and exemptions, streets and sidewalks, economic development, fire, among others. Through the creation of separate zoning codes for Fire Island, the Towns of Islip and Brookhaven recognize that development patterns must be uniquely suited to the natural and cultural character of the Island. Permitted development types are mostly residential, single-family structures designed to minimally impact the beach environment. This type of development induces different transportation needs, such as facilitating pedestrian modes and reducing freight and commercial traffic, than do more intensive land uses and building types.

Both Islip and Brookhaven have adopted zoning codes that have been approved by the Secretary of the Interior as being consistent with Federal standards.[10] The Town of Islip designates its "Residence BAA District" to provide for development that considers the natural function of the barrier island and its ecological systems. The BAA District permits single-family dwellings, municipal uses, and public schools by right, and other community, office, and small-scale retail uses by special permit. The BAA District also regulates height, floor area ratio (FAR), lot size and setbacks, swimming pools, and other site improvements.[11] The Code contains Special Regulations for property in the Fire Island National Seashore, including signs and special permit procedures, that are consistent with NPS standards. Chapter 61 of the Islip Code regulates vehicular uses on Fire Island, including permitting requirements and enforcement.[12]

The Town of Brookhaven has a Residential District (RD), an Oceanfront Dune District (OFD), and a Commercial District (CD) specific to Fire Island. The districts have regulations pertaining to permitted uses, dimensional requirements, signs, fences, accessory buildings, lighting, and swimming pools. Brookhaven also requires each community to establish an advisory committee to monitor development, ensure compliance with regulations to protect the beach, and advise the Town of Brookhaven regarding development.[13]

The Villages of Saltaire and Ocean Beach have their own codes, which include zoning districts, dimensional requirements, signs, fences, docks, swimming pools, and other development standards. Codes also include general governance regulations and procedures, ranging from use and storage of wagons to harbor management.

Fire Island is also influenced by larger regional planning efforts, although many of these efforts have been sparse in recent decades. The Long Island Regional Planning Council, which was established under New York state law to consider regional issues, produced several documents in the 1980s that influenced the management framework for the barrier island. The Hurricane Damage and Mitigation Plan, published in 1984, makes development recommendations to protect shoreline communities from hurricane damage and offers redevelopment strategies in the case of major damage. The Long Island South Shore Hazard Management Program, which was published in 1989, discusses and inventories shoreline structure extent in Nassau and Suffolk Counties, including typical methods of beach stabilization in Fire Island.[14]

---

[10] The Secretary of the Interior approved all four zoning authorities on Fire Island, including Islip and Brookhaven, in 1985, noting several "exceptions" intended to be reviewed on a case-by-case basis.

[11] Town of Islip Code, Chapter 68-135 to Chapter 68-149.5. All Islip Codes accessible at http://www.ecode360.com/?custid=IS0324 (accessed March 22, 2010).

[12] Town of Islip Code, Chapter 68-427 to Chapter 68-432; Chapter 61.

[13] Town of Brookhaven Code, Chapter 85-165 to Chapter 85-182. All Brookhaven Codes accessible at http://www.ecode360.com/?custid=BR0012 (accessed September 14, 2009).

[14] Koppelman, Lee E. and DeWitt Davies. 1984. *Hurricane Damage Mitigation Plan for the South Shore of Nassau and Suffolk Counties, New York*. Long Island Regional Planning Board.
Koppelman, Lee E. and DeWitt Davies. 1989. *Proposed Long Island South Shore Hazard Management Program*. Long Island Regional Planning Board.

Real Estate and Growth Trends

Development patterns on Fire Island influence how many people live and work on the Island as well as how they travel between destinations. The fact that Fire Island is generally built-out, with rising home prices and limited opportunity for redevelopment, is a strong determinant of the types of resident that compose the Island's year-round and seasonal populations. For example, the trend towards older and wealthier residents has coincided with less late-night and lateral ferry demand.

The vast majority of buildings on Fire Island are privately-owned, single-family residences. Lot size varies by community, ranging from one-tenth of an acre to one-quarter of an acre. Table 1 shows an approximate count of all structures by community; structures that far exceeded the average size of structures within a given community are noted separately. The table is based on geographic information systems (GIS) data provided by NPS. Communities with the greatest number of structures are Ocean Beach, Fire Island Pines, Fair Harbor, Saltaire, and Seaview. The total number of structures recorded is 3,878. The total number of structures recorded in the Ethnographic Overview and Assessment was 4,100[15]. Table 1 also includes summer population estimates, which are explained in further detail later in this chapter.

Most houses are wooden structures that are elevated to protect against storm surges, though exceptions exist. The average home price on Fire Island varies by community, with average home values ranging from $200,000 to $750,000. The 2000 Census noted that the median house price on Fire Island is $272,000.

There is little land available on the Island for new housing growth, and this scarcity of new homes reinforces high home prices. Privately owned land is essentially built-out, with only a few unimproved housing lots remaining. NPS staff notes a trend of building larger houses on vacant or "tear-down" lots rather than building two smaller houses on such lots.[16] Population growth is also limited by primitive septic systems, which have little additional capacity.

Residential properties far outnumber commercial properties on Fire Island, with the primary areas of commercial development located in Ocean Beach and Cherry Grove. Smaller commercial real estate clusters include restaurants in Fire Island Pines, the Inn and the Out in Kismet, a bar area adjacent to the Ocean Bay Park marina, and the Davis Park Casino, which contains a large restaurant and bar.

---

[15] 2005. Ethnographic Overview and Assessment, 1.
GIS data provided by National Park Service.
[16] NPS staff also observe that Fire Island homeowners sometimes buy two adjacent lots to build even larger homes, in cases where circumstances and finances allow.

Table 1
Structures Sorted by Community
Source: NPS and Volpe Center

Community	Structures	Large Structures	Seasonal Population Estimate[17]
Atlantique	51		255 – 306
Bluepoint Beach	10		50 – 60
Cherry Grove	259	2	1,295 – 1,554
Cornielle Estates	47	1	235 – 282
Davis Park	273	1	1,365 – 1,638
Dunewood	94	1	470 – 564
Fair Harbor	369		1,845 – 2,214
Fire Island Pines	531	11	2,655 – 3,186
Kismet	210		1,050 – 1,260
Lonelyville	88		440 – 528
Oakleyville	10		50 – 60
Ocean Bay Park	299	2	1,495 – 1,794
Ocean Beach	558	4	2,790 – 3,348
Point O' Woods	153		765 – 918
Robbins Rest	37	1	185 – 222
Saltaire	385	5	1,925 – 2,310
Seaview	373		1,865 – 2,238
Fire Island Summer Club	67		335 – 402
Water Island	35	1	175 – 210
Total	3,849	29	19,245 – 23,094

Communities

The 2005 Ethnographic Overview and Assessment was a NPS-sponsored effort to document the historic, cultural, and social stories and attributes of Fire Island, including characterizations of the Island's 17 communities. As captured in the Ethnographic Overview and Assessment, residents on Fire Island strongly value a relaxed, beach-oriented culture and an escape from the commotion of urban life. Many communities are similar in appearance and share similar challenges with management, natural resources, and conflicts between user groups. Despite their similarities, communities also cling to their independence and residents tend to stay within their communities.

The western communities differ from the eastern in terms of physical layout, travel patterns, population density, and activities.[18] Western communities on the whole are more densely settled, with approximately 2,750 buildings in the western communities and approximately 1,130 in the eastern communities; nearly all the year-round residents live in the western communities. The surface infrastructure in the western

---

[17] These numbers are based on multiplying the number of structures in a community by the average household size of three to four persons, anecdotally noted from stakeholder groups.

[18] Generally the division between eastern and western communities occurs around Sailors Haven. However, driving to communities between Robbins Rest and Point O'Woods requires sufficient additional time that these communities exhibit some characteristics of eastern communities, although their overall layout and travel patterns are more like western communities.

communities more easily accommodates vehicles, leading to much more reliance on driving for basic services such as garbage collection. The eastern communities meet most of their transportation needs by water, and therefore have a more remote and quiet nature. A brief characterization of each community follows, from west to east, based on in-depth research conducted during the 2004 Ethnographic Overview and Assessment.

- **Kismet** is a densely-settled community of single-family residences and rental properties, a small downtown with two restaurants (The Inn and The Out) and two retail shops, and a community playground. The community has paved walks with some boardwalks and a ferry terminal. This residential community is the closest to the Robert Moses Causeway and has the most year-round residents that work on Long Island.
- **Saltaire** is less densely populated than other communities due to zoning requirements and the presence of wetlands. Saltaire lies in the widest part of the Island, and its amenities include churches, a yacht club, a bay beach, a softball field, a small commercial area (with no public restaurants), and a Village Hall containing a library. Nearly all walks are wooden boardwalks, though a few east-west walks accommodate vehicles.
- **Fair Harbor** is dominated by modest bungalows with a range of age and styles densely concentrated around concrete walks and boardwalks. The small commercial district includes a yacht club, a bay beach, and retail shops. Fair Harbor has blue-collar roots and is a popular destination for Long Islanders, and many of its homes are owner-occupied during at least part of the summer.
- **Dunewood** is a small, built-out community with approximately 100 lots, many of which are occupied by original 1950s contemporary one-story homes. The homes are arranged around four north-south concrete walks. Most homes are seasonally owner-occupied by New York metropolitan area residents. The community has abundant vegetation, a yacht club, a small bay beach, and no commercial services.
- **Lonelyville** houses are laid out around sand and wooden walks in a non-grid formation. Lonelyville lacks a large ferry landing, a commercial district, and a bulkhead to stabilize the bayside shore; instead the community has three small finger piers and uses alternative erosion control methods, such as grass planting, a wooden-plank wall, and bales of organic material. There is a high proportion of year-round residents; quiet and privacy are valued.
- **Atlantique** includes a private residential community and a public beach and marina owned and operated by the Town of Islip. Atlantique has a small number of homes arranged around four north-south boardwalks, an informal bay beach, and few year-round families. It houses the Appalachian Mountain Club's Fire Island Cabin, a hostel for AMC members. Atlantique Beach contains play facilities, a bay beach, bathhouse facilities, and numerous organized activities.
- **Robbins Rest** is a small residential community with two north-south boardwalks surrounded on both sides by NPS lands. The bulkhead and small marina are owned by the Robbins Rest Community Association. The community has a small restaurant, bar, and hotel complex but no public ferry service.
- **Fire Island Summer Club** is a private-owned community with a yacht club, tennis court, and bay beach area only accessible to Summer Club residents. Homes are arranged around concrete walks. Due to its proximity to Ocean Beach, its residents often walk there for commercial services and amenities. This is often considered one of Fire Island's more prestigious communities.
- **Cornielle Estates** is a small residential community that has been called a suburb of Ocean Beach due to the close physical and social links between the two communities. The community contains the Woodhull School, a public elementary school serving all of Fire Island.
- **Ocean Beach** is the largest Fire Island community with a mix of historic bungalows and cottages and contemporary larger homes built on pilings. This "metropolis of Fire Island"[19] has a large, commercial district that serves as a social center and attracts people from many surrounding communities. The public Ocean Beach Community House, a boathouse near the ferry dock, and

---

[19] 2005. Ethnographic Overview and Assessment. National Park Service, 184.

other outdoor spaces hosts regular social events and concerts. The community has many year-round residents.
- **Seaview** is a predominantly residential community with larger lots arranged around a concrete walk grid and a contemporary, affluent appearance. The community is highly vegetated and contains a small public park, a small commercial area, a marina, a large bay beach, and a ball field. Seaview has two synagogues and a very large Jewish population. Residents call it a quiet, family community.
- **Ocean Bay Park** has long been popular with group renters for its festive atmosphere, facilitated by the presence of several restaurants and bars, though some observe that group rentals have decreased recently. The community has higher residential density and a continuation of the concrete walk grid. The community attracts visitors from nearby communities who come to enjoy the nightlife. There is also a large family contingent, including a few year-round residents.
- All land in **Point O' Woods** is owned by the Point O' Woods Association. Residents own their homes, some of the largest on the Island, and have long-term leases on the underlying land. The street pattern follows the topography of the dunes, rather than a grid, and the community has several social and recreational amenities, including a popular yacht club. Point O' Woods is an exclusive, gated community that is closed to pass-through traffic. The community is highly vegetated with a large amount of open green space, and it also has a unique narrow-gauge railway connecting the ferry dock to the Clubhouse.
- **Cherry Grove** is the oldest continually-inhabited community, densely filled with modest cottages, with a mostly gay population. The community is heavily vegetated and contains only wooden boardwalks that cannot accommodate vehicles. A lively commercial district attracts crowds from neighboring communities and Long Island.
- **Fire Island Pines** is the second-largest community with large, often contemporary homes along shaded, wooden boardwalks and sand drives. Houses and landscaping tend to be more lavish. The commercial area clusters around a dock and a small marina. Residents tend to be affluent, artistic, and gay, and the culture is social but more subdued than Cherry Grove.
- **Water Island** is a small residential community with traditional and modestly designed homes around boardwalks and a simple ferry dock. Houses are mostly owner-occupied, and the community is described as quiet and family-oriented. There are no year-round residents.
- **Davis Park** is the eastern-most community, attracting mostly Long Island residents. A small commercial area is clustered around the marina and ferry dock, although the Davis Park Casino (a popular bar/restaurant destination) lies closer to the ocean. All walks are sand and boardwalks. The community attracts numerous day-trippers but seasonal visitors also include homeowners, renters, and boaters.

Population

Fire Island differs from many other NPS sites due to the presence of robust seasonal and year-round populations. The year-round population is estimated at approximately 500 residents, based on the number of vehicle permits issued to year-round residents and the Census 2000 population data. As depicted in Table 1, seasonal residents are estimated to number between 19,000 and 23,000. This estimate is calculated by multiplying the number of structures on Fire Island by the average household size.[20]

Seasonal and year-round residents form two distinct groups, both in terms of their socioeconomic backgrounds and their perspectives about transportation on Fire Island. The majority of seasonal residents maintain permanent residences on Long Island or in metropolitan New York City, according to

---

[20] The number of structures on the Island is likely between 3,800 and 4,100 (based on NPS GIS data and the EO&A), with most structures being residential. The average household size is estimated to range from 5 to 6 persons, given the popularity of the Island with families and group renters. While some households have rotating groups of tenants, the estimate accounts for the number of seasonal residents on Fire Island on any given weekend during the summer season. It should also be noted that certain communities (including Ocean Bay Park) have more group rental homes than others, and the average household size is larger in these communities.

the results of a 2000 survey conducted by the Volpe Center[21]. Some seasonal residents travel to Fire Island for periods of several weeks or months, whereas others use their Fire Island residence primarily on weekends and travel back to their permanent residence during the week. The large number of seasonal residents traveling on Fridays and Sundays results in very heavy ferry traffic on those days.

Owners of rental properties on Fire Island may lease their homes by the week, month, or season, resulting in a populace that is transient throughout the summer season. The rental season runs from May 15 through September 15, and attracts a large number of families with school-age children. Shoulder-season rentals (April through May and September through November) are increasing with retirees and families with non-school-age children. The influx of seasonal residents leads to vastly different conditions for transportation during the summer months.

Several community associations have regulations dictating the leasing of homes to manage noise and the provision of public services. In recent years, NPS staff observed a shift in seasonal residents and renters towards families and smaller parties. Previously, large groups of young adults (with and without children) would share one rental house to cover high rent. Some community associations began to discourage these group renters due to noise complaints and strains on community resources, and homeowners became more reluctant to risk property damage by renting to groups. The result has been a wealthier rental population, including affluent young families, and more retirees. In other cases, several families will rent a house together and use the house during different weeks.

As real estate prices rise, Fire Island homeowners are becoming increasingly older and wealthier, which will affect future transportation needs. Home prices that were historically affordable to middle-class New Yorkers are now more exclusively within the means of more affluent people. Long-time Fire Island residents who have kept their homes tend to be older, and new residents tend to have higher incomes. Elderly residents may have reduced mobility, necessitating special golf carts to help them get around their communities. Some communities, such as Water Island, may be too challenging for residents with physical limitations to traverse. Older residents may also be less able to help out with firefighting and other essential community services. The new, wealthier residents demand different types of transportation, as well. Contractors report that these residents request major contracting services, including large-scale home renovations and landscaping, requiring the transport of more materials to Fire Island.

Most year-round residents live in Ocean Beach, Fair Harbor, and Saltaire, though year-round residential driving permits have been issued to residents in every community except Water Island. Like with the seasonal population, the proportion of elderly year-round residents is increasing. Year-round residents emphasize the importance of families permanently living on the Island, both to maintain the sense of community and also to provide basic services. Year-round residents have different transportation needs and different transportation resources available to them. During the off-season, there is reduced demand for ferry service as well as climatic limitations to water-based transport, such as ice in the Great South Bay. Services such as power, water, phone service, garbage disposal, boardwalk maintenance, and general contracting for private homes occur throughout the year, though the transportation systems to support such services vary by season.

A key service provided for year-round residents is school-related transport. The Fire Island School District, which is a public school district serving all of Fire Island, currently operates an elementary school for grades pre-Kindergarten through 6 with 29 students enrolled for the 2009-2010 school year. The District also pays tuition for 29 students to attend middle schools and high schools on Long Island. Additionally, five students attend parochial school on Long Island. The School District provides transportation for all 61 students. A detailed description of this service appears in Chapter 5.

---

[21] Volpe National Transportation Systems Center. 2001. "Fire Island National Seashore Waterborne Transportation System Plan." U.S. Department of Transportation.

Both seasonal and year-round residents tend to stay primarily within their communities, especially during the summer months where congestion limits lateral island travel. The main exception is contractors, who use permitted vehicles to travel to job sites across the Island and to exchange materials on Long Island. Short-term visitors, those who stay for one week or less, tend to move between communities and NPS sites.

Section 3: Transportation Overview

The transportation systems on and around Fire Island employ a unique mix of water- and land-based travel modes. The roadless character of the Island, its multiple gateway access points, and its proximity to the New York metropolitan area help dictate the formation and operation of these transportation systems on Fire Island.

Mainland Connections

Most visitors accessing Fire Island must first travel to a Fire Island access point either by car or by rail. The road-based access points are the Robert Moses Causeway and the William Floyd Parkway, and the water-based access points include ferry terminals in Bay Shore, Sayville, and Patchogue.

The Robert Moses Causeway is classified as a Principal Arterial (Expressway). The road segment where the Causeway enters Robert Moses State Park had an average daily traffic count of 15,600 in 2002, though the data does not indicate the time of year that the traffic count was recorded.[22] The Causeway connects Robert Moses State Park and the western access point for FIIS with five major highways: State Route 27A (Montauk Highway), State Route 27 (Sunrise Highway), the Southern State Parkway, and the Northern State Parkway. These roads offer connections to Long Island, New York City, and New England. Visitors who drive to the west end of Fire Island may park at one of several fee-based parking lots at Robert Moses State Park. The closest of these to the National Seashore is the Field 5 parking lot, which has 2,460 spaces that fill during the summer (there is a total of 8,200 parking spaces among the four parking fields in the State Park).

The William Floyd Parkway (County Route 46) is classified as a Principal Arterial (Other Street). It had an average daily traffic count of 24,744 accessing Smith Point County Park, based on a count taken in July 2007 (most recent data available on Suffolk County website).[23] It connects Smith Point County Park and the eastern access point for FIIS with the eastern portion of Long Island, including the William Floyd Estate. The William Floyd Parkway intersects with S.R. 27 and with Interstate 495. Visitors driving to the east side of Fire Island must park at the 4,000 space parking lot at Smith Point County Park, where a fee is collected by Suffolk County.

Many visitors also use private vehicles to access ferry terminals at Bay Shore, Sayville, or Patchogue. Each of the gateway communities directly links to S.R. 27A and is easily accessible from I-495 and several other major regional arterials. Ferry companies provide fee-based parking lots, including overnight parking, for ferry passengers. The NPS Patchogue Ferry Terminal, serving Watch Hill, offers free parking for passengers.

Visitors may also access ferry terminals via the Long Island Railroad. The Babylon Branch of the LIRR begins service at Jamaica Station in Queens.[24] At Babylon Station, the Babylon Branch changes to the Montauk Branch, which serves Bay Shore, Sayville, Patchogue, and other points east along the South Shore. The Patchogue LIRR station is located one-quarter mile from the NPS Ferry Terminal and one mile from the Davis Park Ferry Terminal. The Bay Shore LIRR station is located approximately three miles from the ferry terminal, and the Sayville LIRR station is located approximately 1.5 miles from the ferry terminal. Private taxi services shuttle passengers between the LIRR stations and the Bay Shore and Sayville ferry terminals, as ferry schedules are coordinated to accommodate LIRR arrivals and departures.

---

[22] New York Department of Transportation. 2010. "Traffic Data." Highway Data Services. Accessed 23 March 2010: https://www.nysdot.gov/divisions/engineering/technical-services/highway-data-services.

[23] Suffolk County Department of Public Works. 2007. "Traffic Volume Counts." Accessed 29 March 2010: http://www.co.suffolk.ny.us/departments/publicworks/trafficcounts.aspx.

[24] Jamaica Station is directly accessible from LIRR's major transit hubs, Penn Station in Manhattan and Flatbush Avenue/Brooklyn Station in Brooklyn. Travelers from Penn Station and Flatbush Avenue/Brooklyn Station generally have to make one transfer at Jamaica to get to LIRR stations that access Fire Island.

Public transit provides another means for visitors to reach Fire Island. Suffolk County Transit operates three bus routes that offer access to Fire Island or to FIIS visitation areas. Routes 7E and S66 both run along Neighborhood Road and Mastic Beach Road in Mastic Beach, and the routes pass within 0.8 miles of the entrance to William Floyd Estate. Service for the 7E line is approximately every 1.5 hours between 7:30 a.m. to 6:30 p.m. The S66 line, which connects Patchogue and Riverhead, runs from 5:30 a.m. to 7:30 p.m. and operates approximately once an hour. Both lines run Monday through Saturday, excluding major holidays. During the summer (June through September), the 7E line also runs to Smith Point County Park every 1.5 hours between 10 a.m. and 6 p.m. Visitors could then walk approximately one-quarter mile to the Fire Island Wilderness Visitor Center. Suffolk County Transit also operates bus route S47, which runs seasonally to Robert Moses State Park and stops at the Field 3 parking area. The bus stop at Field 3 is a 2.6 mile walk to the Fire Island Lighthouse Visitor Center. The S47 bus runs every 30 to 60 minutes between 9 a.m. and 7 p.m. from late June through early September, including weekends and holidays. The one-way fare for Suffolk County Transit is $1.50.

Finally, several nearby airports offer air-based connections for visitors traveling greater distances. Patchogue and Sayville are both located within five miles of Long Island Islip MacArthur Airport, a public commercial airport served by U.S. Airways and Southwest Airlines. Fire Island is also accessible from LaGuardia International Airport and John F. Kennedy International Airport via train and private vehicle connections.

Marine Transportation

Fire Island's three passenger ferry companies are responsible for transporting nearly all of the Island's residents, visitors, and workers and much of their cargo from Long Island gateways to Fire Island:

- From Bay Shore. Fire Island Ferries serves the communities of Kismet, Saltaire (*), Fair Harbor (*), Dunewood, Atlantique, Atlantique Beach, Ocean Beach (*),Seaview, and Ocean Bay Park (*). *An asterisk (*) indicates year-round service, weather permitting.*
- From Sayville. Sayville Ferry serves the communities of Cherry Grove, Fire Island Pines, and Water Island (service operates year-round during weekends only, weather permitting; no winter service to Water Island), as well as the Sailors Haven Visitor Center under a NPS contract (seasonal service).
- From Patchogue. Davis Park Ferry serves the community of Davis Park and the Watch Hill Visitor Center, the latter under a NPS contract. These ferry services operate out of two different ferry terminals, located in different locations on the Patchogue River.

Two private cross-bay ferries offer service restricted to residents of specific communities. Point O' Woods has a private ferry service exclusive to residents, operating from a Bay Shore terminal adjacent to the Fire Island Ferries terminals. The Village of Bellport (on Long Island) operates a private ferry to Bellport Beach, a village-owned beach within the Otis Pike Wilderness area open to Bellport residents only.

In addition to cross-bay passenger ferries, several other types of boats bring people and goods to and around Fire Island. Each of the three passenger ferry companies also owns and operates freight barges to the communities that they serve. Additionally, several companies exclusively operate freight barges, including Tony's Barge and Coastline Freight. These freight barges haul garbage, commercial construction materials, propane tanks, and other large freight to Fire Island destinations. Fire Island Ferries operates Fire Island Water Taxi, a lateral water transport service that provides on-demand trips among most Fire Island communities and NPS sites. Finally, many visitors, residents, and workers access Fire Island via private boat. Several communities and NPS sites have marinas to accommodate private vessels, although slips fill quickly during peak summer periods.

Fire Island Infrastructure

Vehicular and Pedestrian Access

While Fire Island is officially "roadless" in nature, the Island contains a network of boardwalks, concrete walks, and sand roads that accommodate vehicles, pedestrians, and bicyclists. Figures 4, 5, and 6 illustrate the walks and paths that can be used for vehicular transport on Fire Island.

The principal east-west route transecting the Island is known as Burma Road, though it goes by different names in individual communities and was formerly known as the Coast Guard Road. The Burma Road is predominantly a sand and gravel road, although many sections that run through communities on the western section of Fire Island have been paved. The road also serves as the utility corridor for the Island with several utility lines buried beneath it and utility poles overhead. The Burma Road ends at the western boundary of the Otis Pike Wilderness, where both motorized and non-motorized vehicles are prohibited. Permitted vehicles and UTVs can drive along the Burma Road for inland travel during times when tides or habitat restrictions limit beach travel, except in Cherry Grove and Water Island where inland vehicle travel cannot be accommodated by boardwalk infrastructure at any time. As observed during site visits and relayed by NPS staff, drivers tend to avoid the Burma Road for east-west vehicular movement because it is generally considered to be a slower route than the beach. Pedestrians also use the Burma Road and other inland sand routes to walk between communities or to access NPS sites.

Within the communities, wooden boardwalks form the primary transportation network to accommodate pedestrian traffic. In most communities, boardwalks run north to south, connecting the ocean beach with the Great South Bay. In addition to the boardwalks, some communities (Kismet, Saltaire, Fair Harbor, Dunewood, Robbins Rest, Fire Island Summer Club, Cornielle Estates, Ocean Beach, Seaview, and Ocean Bay Park) also have concrete walks running east-west; these walks may be part of the Burma Road or other east-west routes connecting the wooden boardwalks. The communities of Kismet, Fair Harbor, Dunewood, Fire Island Summer Club, Ocean Beach, Seaview, and Ocean Bay Park also have north-south concrete walks and do not have wooden boardwalks. Other communities have primarily sand paths that accommodate limited vehicle traffic alongside boardwalks for pedestrian traffic. Generally, cars are restricted to the concrete walks or sand routes, while pedestrians may use concrete walks or boardwalks. One exception is Saltaire, where a few boardwalks can accommodate vehicles.

The ocean beaches are a primary access route for east-west travel around Fire Island. Vehicles with NPS-issued permits may drive on the beach during driving season (or year-round for emergency services and essential services) and in compliance with the "Rhizome Rule". The Rhizome Rule dictates that drivers must stay at least 20 feet seaward of the toe of the dunes or visible beach grass at all times; if 20 feet of beach is not available between the toe of the dune and the water's edge, motor vehicle travel is prohibited on the beach. Some parts of the beach are permanently closed to vehicles, including Lighthouse Beach and Sailors Haven Beach. A portion of the beach from Long Cove to South Point is closed temporarily due to nesting plovers. Inland routes (via the Burma Road) are maintained in these areas to accommodate motor vehicle travel. NPS also closes portions of other beaches on Federal lands as needed to protect natural resources, as called for in the Endangered Species Management Plan.[25]

Walking is the most popular means of travel on Fire Island. Concrete walks, boardwalks, and sand walks are all primarily designed to accommodate pedestrians and allow them to safely and easily access beaches, ferry docks, residences, and other destinations. These walking paths appear in Figures 4, 5, and 6, with thicker lines denoting primary travel routes. Primary travel routes have higher volumes of pedestrian (and sometimes vehicular) trips, as indicated by the presence of key community amenities and confirmed by observations of NPS staff. Most vehicular/pedestrian conflicts are avoided by prohibiting or severely

---

[25] Negotiated Rulemaking Advisory Committee for Off-Road Driving Regulations at Fire Island National Seashore. 2003. "Final Consensus Agreement." 22 August. Accessible at http://www.nps.gov/archive/fiis/negreg/FI_8-22-03_FinalCD.pdf.

limiting driving during the summer season and shoulder season weekends, when pedestrian traffic is heaviest.

On most parts of Fire Island, the beach is the most popular pedestrian route for lateral travel. In areas where soft sand paths are the only means of lateral inland travel, the firm sand near the ocean is a more pleasant walking surface for trips of any distance. Walking along the beach is also a very popular recreational activity, with no specific lateral destination.

NPS also maintains several trails for recreational and transportation use. A 1.5 mile wooden boardwalk at Sailors Haven allows visitors to view the Sunken Forest, a rare maritime holly forest. Another popular pedestrian route on Federal lands is a one-mile paved walkway, separated from the Burma Road, that connects the Sailors Haven Visitor Center with the community of Cherry Grove. There are also short sand and boardwalk nature trails at the Fire Island Lighthouse Visitor Center and the Fire Island Wilderness Visitor Center, Watch Hill, and Talisman. Hikers may traverse the Otis Pike Wilderness along sand paths or along the beach, though these are not formally maintained as pedestrian transportation facilities. NPS trails are shown in green on Figures 5 and 6.

Figure 4
Transportation Networks: Robert Moses S.P. to Atlantique
Source: Volpe Center

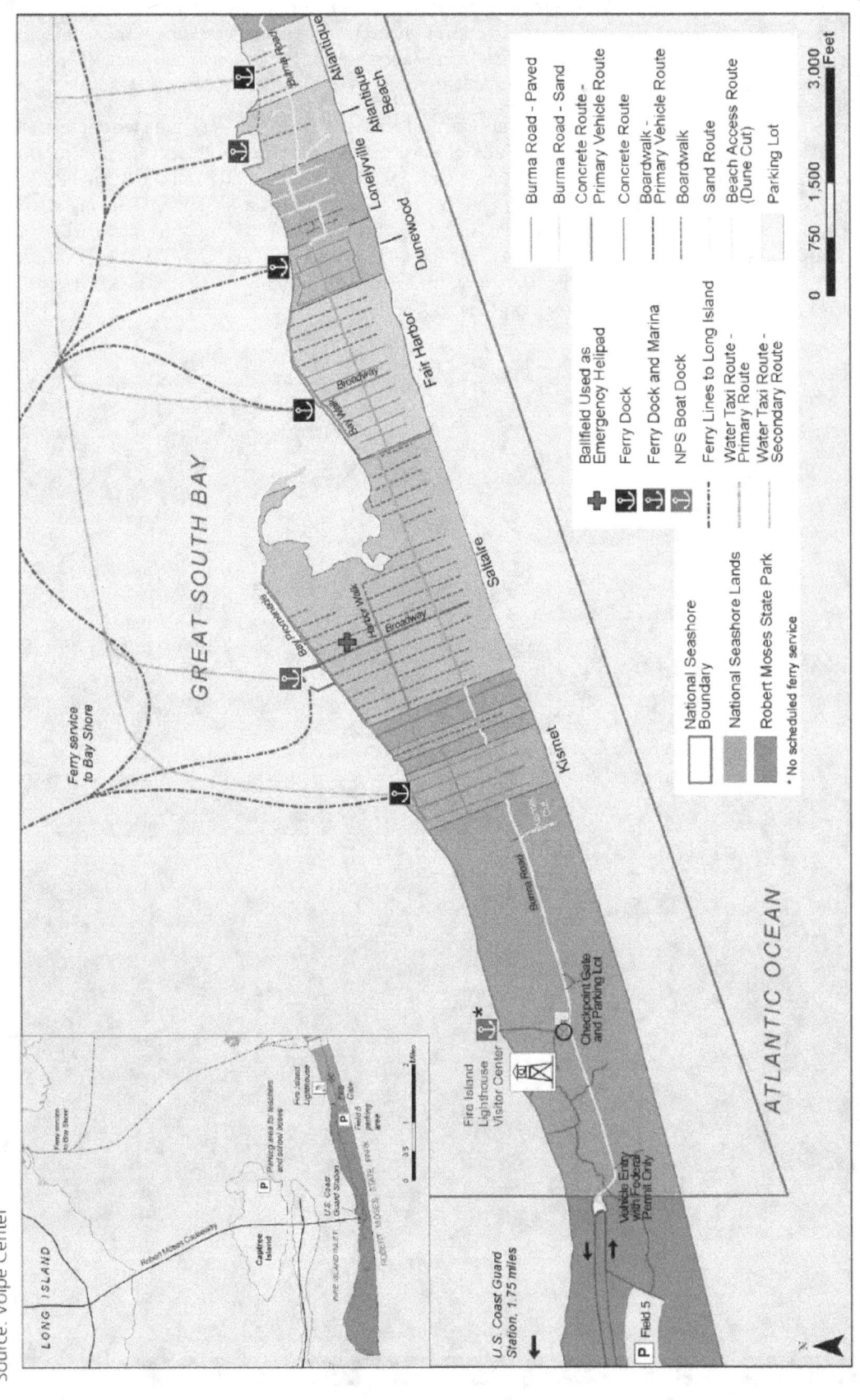

Figure 5
Transportation Networks: Robbins Rest to Point O Woods
Source: Volpe Center

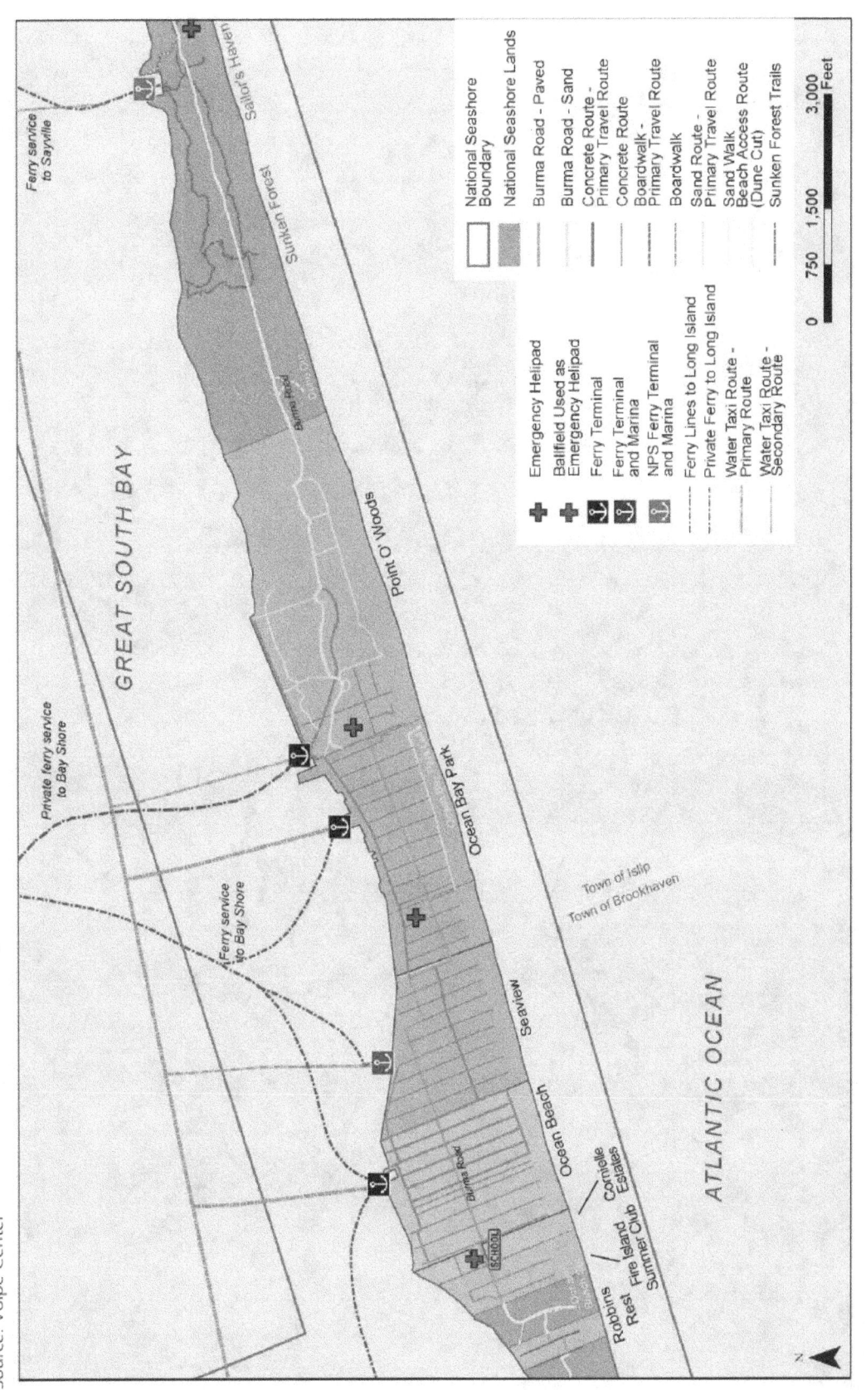

Fire Island National Seashore – Alternative Transportation Study

Figure 6
Transportation Networks: Cherry Grove to Watch Hill
Source: Volpe Center

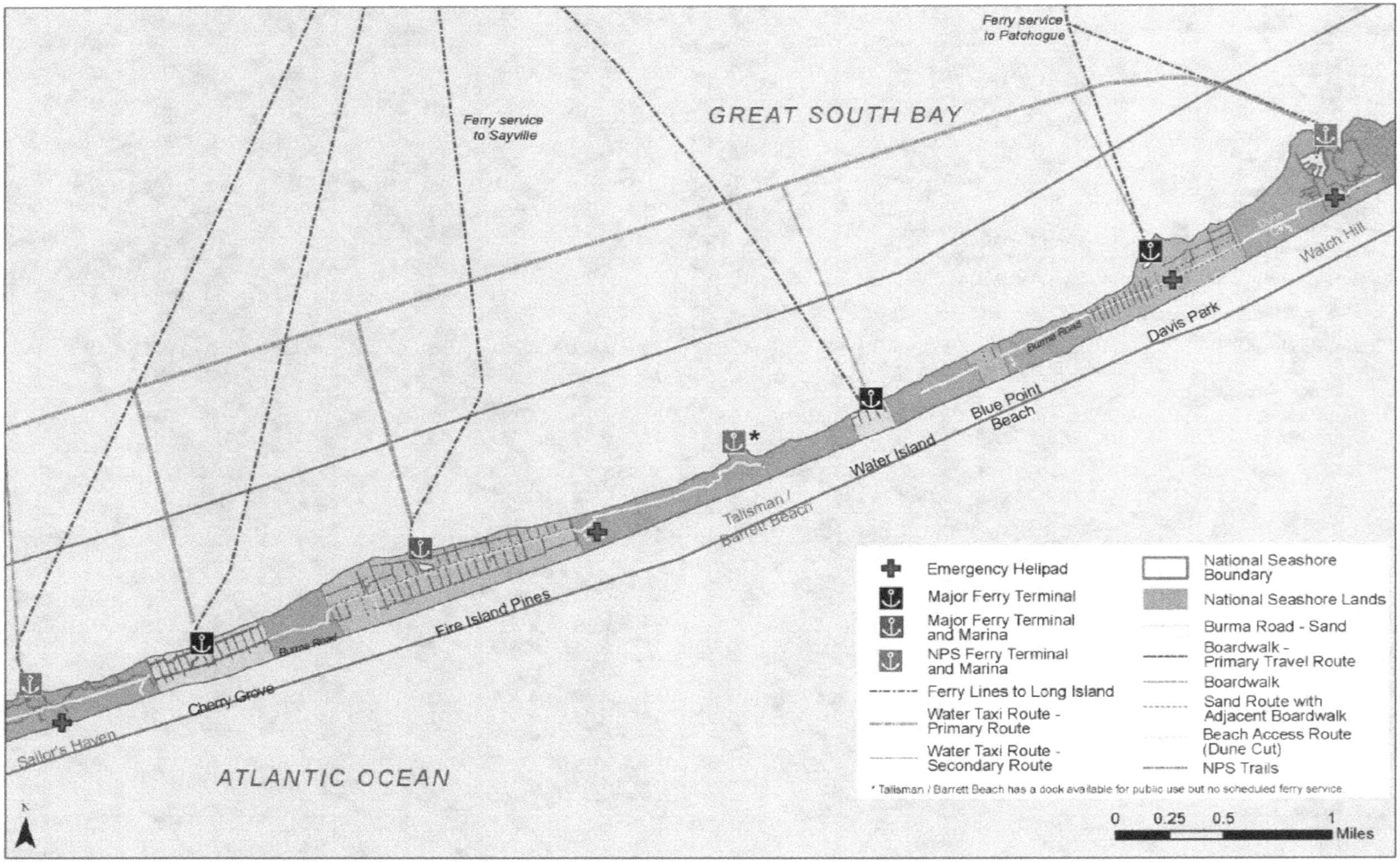

Bicycle Access

Bicycling is a travel mode that is well-accommodated on some parts of Fire Island and prohibited in others. While several barriers offer challenges to bicyclists, many visitors and workers still use bicycles as a primary means of transport.

Visitors who wish to ride bicycles on Fire Island must bring them onto the Island either on a ferry or via the western FIIS gate at the Fire Island Lighthouse Center. Bicyclists may ride over the bridge to Smith Point County Park. The eastern NPS gate leads to the Otis Pike Wilderness, where bicycles are prohibited. Bicycles are also prohibited from the Robert Moses Causeway, so visitors must use a private vehicle to drive bicycles to a parking area in Robert Moses State Park, where bike riding is also prohibited The route between the western NPS gate and Kismet is made of sand and crushed shell, but despite the unpaved surface, the route is popular with bicyclists who ride from the Field 5 parking lot to the western communities. There is no designated bicycle path in Fire Island National Seashore, but bikes may be used on designated off-road vehicle routes. Biking on the beach is permissible.

Contractors, some utilities, and other employees who work regularly on Fire Island drive vehicles carrying bicycles to Field 5 and commute by bicycle to their work site. Anecdotally, these employees report that this bicycling method of commuting is faster and provides them with greater independence than taking a ferry.

Ferry company policies do not permit carriage of bicycles to the Island. Fire Island Ferries carts bicycles separately on freight ferries (for a cost of $4 for children's bicycles and $5 for adult bicycles). Sayville Ferry and Davis Park Ferry operators note that the communities they serve either do not or cannot accommodate bicycles so they will not permit them aboard their ferries.

Communities on Fire Island vary in their rules about bicycle use. Bicycling is a primary mode of transportation in some communities with lots of concrete walks. Many communities prohibit bicycle use on boardwalks, after dark, and/or during summer weekends; reasons for the prohibitions include narrow and elevated boardwalks. During the summer season, Ocean Beach prohibits bicycles on Bayview Walk between Ocean Road and Surf View Walk on weekends and during the evenings; bikes are permitted any time during off season except on holidays. The Town of Brookhaven prohibits bicycle use on boardwalks. This stipulation effectively prohibits bicycle use community-wide in Cherry Grove, Fire Island Pines, Water Island and Davis Park, where the only pathways are boardwalks or soft sand, although some bicyclists do bike on sand paths.

Sections 4 and 5 describe how those who live and work on Fire Island employ water- and vehicular-based transportation systems to meet their mobility needs. The sections are organized by mode and by user group, reflecting two of the most influential factors in Fire Island travel.

Section 4: Water-based Transport

Overview

The policy of the Fire Island National Seashore is to maximize the use of water transport, including in situations where land transport options exist. The towns and incorporated villages support this approach, by and large, through regulation and practice. As a result, the transportation system is a complex array of boats and barges that can accommodate a diversity of passengers and cargo to meet the needs of Fire Island residents and visitors. Water-based transport is highly dependent on seasonal demand and weather conditions, although generally some level of water-based service is available year-round. The water-based transport consists of passenger ferries, freight ferries, garbage and other special barges, water taxi for lateral movement, and private boats. Water-based transportation is also reliant upon on-island infrastructure of parking, docks and marinas to facilitate the connection of people and goods from their origins to their final destinations.

Image 1
Ferry Departing Ocean Bay Park
Source: Volpe Center

Passenger Ferries

Three ferry companies offer passenger service to the general public, and another two ferry companies serve specific, restricted passenger routes. NPS does not regulate any of the passenger or freight ferries, with the exception of setting contract agreements for passenger ferry service to NPS sites. However, since ferries operate in waters under NPS jurisdiction, NPS has the authority to regulate the ferries.

The schedules of the three passenger ferry companies are very similar but operate ten to fifteen minutes apart because of their close linkages with the LIRR schedule. Coordination with the rail schedule is a high priority for ferry operators to accommodate residents and visitors from New York City, although some ferry operators have anecdotally observed a decline in passengers traveling by LIRR in recent years. Ferries operate on a minimal schedule during winter months, with cross-bay service stopping for weeks at a time due to inclement weather or ice on the bay. During periods when ferries are not operating, Fire Island residents or contractors without year-round driving permits connect with other residents or contractors with permits to carpool on and off the Island.

Round-trip adult ferry fares range from approximately $12 to $17 during the summer season, with discounts for children, seniors, and bulk purchasers. Fare increases for ferry companies must be submitted to Suffolk County for a formal six-month review process. County staff undertake a budget review and report to the County Legislature, who make a determination if the fare increase is valid and approvable. Ferry operators note that this process makes it difficult for operators to adjust to fuel price changes.

Fire Island Ferries

Fire Island Ferries operates out of Bay Shore, Long Island. It is the only passenger ferry company offering year-round scheduled passenger service (weather-permitting) and the only company not under contract with NPS. Fire Island Ferries also operates the Fire Island Water Taxi, which is described in greater detail later in this section.

Fire Island Ferries has a fleet of nine boats, built between 1964 and 2001, between 60 and 80 feet in length and 16 to 20 feet in breadth, with capacities between 150 and 395 passengers. Fire Island Ferries allocates boats to certain routes based on demand. One passenger ferry is dedicated full-time to Ocean Beach. A second ferry serves both Saltaire and Kismet, though two separate vessels may serve these communities during peak periods; a similar arrangement exists between Seaview and Ocean Bay Park. Dunewood and Atlantique are always served by one boat; this boat may also serve Fair Harbor during non-peak times. When considering ferry selection, ferry operators try to not run at capacity as doing so may affect the comfort of some passengers. While Fire Island Ferries has considered using smaller, 40-passenger boats (the same boats used for water taxi services) during low-demand periods, operators note that this has not been a high priority as they do not want to be caught without enough capacity to meet demand.

Fire Island Ferries runs two shifts of commuter ferries during the summer, including a 7 a.m. and 8:15 a.m. ferry from Bay Shore and a 4 p.m. and a 5 p.m. ferry from Fire Island. These boats serve waiters, lifeguards, and service employees. The ferry operator also runs a 5 a.m. ferry from Bay Shore during the summer to transport perishable food to the Island; this ferry then leaves Fire Island at 6 a.m. and takes commuters to Long Island to allow them to travel to work in New York City.

Sayville Ferry

Sayville Ferry, operating from Sayville, Long Island, has a fleet of four boats, including two 105-passenger boats built in the 1960s and a 412-passenger boat built in 1996. Ferries are selected for runs according to demand, but generally large boats are used on the weekends and small boats during the week. During periods of high winds or other inclement weather, large boats may be used in place of the smaller boats, regardless of demand, for reasons of safety and comfort.

Sayville Ferry serves Sailors Haven, under contract to NPS, from early May through October. Sayville Ferry also serves Cherry Grove and Fire Island Pines, with daily service through Thanksgiving weekend (weather permitting), and Water Island with weekend service in season. Although regular scheduled service stops by December, Sayville Ferry will run charters by request year-round. The frequency of charter service ranges from daily trips to trips only once every few weeks. Sayville Ferry operators estimate that 80 to 90 percent of their weekday, off-season passengers are contractors commuting to the Island for work. They estimate that 75 percent of passengers on weekends during the off-season are homeowners.

Davis Park Ferry Company

Davis Park Ferry operates services to the Watch Hill Visitor Center and to the community of Davis Park from two different ferry terminals in Patchogue, located approximately three-quarters of a mile apart on the Patchogue River. Service to Watch Hill is under contract to NPS, running from early May through October, and operating from the NPS-owned ferry terminal located one-quarter mile from the Patchogue train station and one-quarter mile from the FIIS headquarters. In the future, this service will operate from the recently-completed NPS ferry terminal building, located adjacent to the existing NPS terminal, and scheduled to be operational starting in May 2010. Neither the existing nor the new terminal, located on

NPS property, charges parking fees, and both permit overnight parking, generally intended for campers staying at Watch Hill.

Watch Hill ferry service generally operates between 10 a.m. and 6 p.m. on weekdays in-season and between 9 a.m. and 7 p.m. on weekends, with a special 10 p.m. ferry scheduled to accommodate Watch Hill restaurant patrons. Davis Park Ferry operators note that ferry ridership to Watch Hill has decreased in recent years, with approximately 26,000 passengers in 2007 and 21,000 passengers in 2009. (Visitation to Watch Hill has not decreased, according to the concessionaire, due to steady numbers of visitors with private boats).

The Davis Park service, through a special use permit with the Town of Brookhaven, has daily scheduled service through the end of October and weekend service through Thanksgiving. The Davis Park Ferry terminal is south of the NPS ferry terminal, near the mouth of the Patchogue River. Parking at the site is free for Brookhaven residents, while other users must pay a fee. Davis Park service operates between the hours of 10 a.m. and 10 p.m., with the last boat leaving Davis Park at 9:30 p.m. in season. A late boat, leaving at 1 a.m., used to be popular but demand has declined drastically in recent years, forcing a cut in service. Most passengers using this site are Long Island residents; there is not sufficient demand for taxi or shuttle connections between the LIRR station and the ferry terminal.

Davis Park Ferry's fleet includes a 49-passenger boat, two 250-passenger boats, and a 300-passenger boat. Ferry operators try to choose the boat size based on passenger demand, but weather sometimes dictates the use of a larger boat for safety reasons.

Very few of Davis Park Ferry's customers are contractors, and ferry demand does not significantly decrease during the driving season. Operators note that most contractors that work in Davis Park have their own boats.

Other Ferries

Two private passenger ferries offer service to Fire Island for designated residents. Point O' Woods Ferry operates one round trip daily between Bay Shore and Point O' Woods. The service is restricted to residents of Point O' Woods. The Bellport Ferry offers seven daily round trips between the Village of Bellport and Bellport Beach (also known as "Ho-hum Beach") on Fire Island. The service operates weekends only from late May through late June and six days a week (excluding Tuesdays, when the beach is closed) from the end of June through Labor Day weekend, with limited, weather-dependent service after Labor Day. The Bellport Ferry is open to Bellport residents and their guests only, with round-trip fares ranging from $4 to $10, depending on age of passenger and day of the week.

Freight

Several companies offer freight services to meet the range of needs for Fire Island residents and services. The three passenger ferry companies operate separate freight boats to carry freight to Fire Island. The ferry operators generally permit passengers to bring two pieces of hand luggage aboard passenger ferries. Any material in excess of this, including oversize items, must be carried by freight boat. Freight boats also accommodate food and merchandise delivery to retailers, furniture and home décor items for residences, groceries for residents, and other cargo that needs to be transported to Fire Island. Freight boat operators are accustomed to meeting special requests; most freight operators offer charters or other accommodations to meet freight needs. During late spring, as contractors and residents prepare homes for the summer season, freight volume is at its height, with individual operators running multiple daily trips, sometimes leading to dock congestion.

Fire Island Ferries runs scheduled freight ferry to Kismet, Saltaire, Fair Harbor, Dunewood, Atlantique, Ocean Beach, Seaview, and Ocean Bay Park. Freight ferries depart from Bay Shore at 10 a.m. Monday through Friday, year-round, weather permitting. Fire Island Ferries also operates a Saturday freight boat from mid-April to mid-October. Service frequency may be adjusted based on demand.

Fire Island Ferries owns and operates three freight boats. The largest freight ferry, the *America*, may make up to three trips a day during peak periods. The vessel serves almost all retailers and restaurants in communities west of Point O' Woods, although there is no refrigerated section for perishable freight. The *Vagabond* is a smaller and older flatbed barge that can accommodate vehicles. Fire Island Ferries also owns an old passenger boat that is currently used to haul pallets.

Four communities (Ocean Beach, Fair Harbor, Seaview, and Ocean Bay Park) served by Fire Island Ferries have freight houses that store freight for owners to retrieve up to seven days later; in these communities, freight owners do not have to be present to meet the freight delivery in their community. Saltaire has a cartage concessionaire who can deliver freight to residences. Freight owners in other communities may add shipping dates to their freight and have it delivered to the Bay Shore terminal up to several days in advance.

Sayville Ferry has a freight boat that runs from April 1 through early November, with up to ten scheduled trips per week in season. Sayville Ferry estimates that 90 to 100 percent of freight coming to Cherry Grove, Fire Island Pines, and Water Island come by water. Sayville Freight only goes to Water Island by charter; there is no regularly-scheduled service. Like Saltaire, Fire Island Pines also has a delivery service to take freight to individual residences. People who want to bring kayaks to Fire Island must send them by freight boat, but Sayville Ferry operators say that they will take kayaks on passenger boats during low-volume trips.

Davis Park owns a freight boat, called "The Turtle," but it runs infrequently and is stored at a separate facility further north on the Patchogue River near the NPS maintenance facility. The Davis Park Ferry freight boat accommodates residential and retail deliveries, but many of the cargo services in Davis Park (including garbage hauling and walk repair) are covered by private operators.

In addition to the freight services of the passenger ferry operators, several freight-specific companies offer service to Fire Island. Tony's Barge, based in Sayville, has approximately three freight boats and barges with capability to haul vehicles, major equipment, and other oversized freight. Tony's Barge serves as the main water-based garbage hauler for all of Fire Island and has municipal waste management contracts with most communities, though a few communities are served by other companies. In addition to owning a fleet of barges, the operator also owns garbage vehicles that circulate within communities and drive off garbage from the western communities. For communities including and east of Ocean Beach, Tony's Barge carries trucks or UTVs (depending on the dock capabilities of each community) to perform curbside garbage pick-up. All municipal waste and the vehicles used for curbside pick-up are then boated back across the bay to Sayville.

Coastline Freight & Charter operates scheduled freight service out of Sayville to Fire Island Pines and Cherry Grove year-round, weather permitting. Freight services to other communities are also available by charter. Coastline has three scheduled trips Tuesdays through Fridays in season, two scheduled trips on Saturdays, and one scheduled trip on Mondays. Coastline also has a daily scheduled trip Mondays through Fridays during the winter, weather permitting. The company offers home delivery, bay front barge service, and storage facilities on Long Island. They have capability to haul lumber and other construction materials.

The Town of Brookhaven also maintains its own ferry facility in Patchogue with a cargo boat that serves the Brookhaven communities. The cargo boat is an LCN landing craft that can haul construction materials and equipment, including vehicles, for boardwalk maintenance. The boat travels to Fire Island approximately five days a week year-round, weather permitting. The barge generally brings at least one vehicle to work on the Island, though Brookhaven will often drive additional vehicles to job sites. The Town owns a second boat, a 31-foot utility boat, which is used to transport employees and some materials. Brookhaven is also able to store materials and equipment at garages in Davis Park and Fire Island Pines, thus reducing their need to haul materials back to Long Island each day.

Two other freight companies also serve the Island. Spoons Carting operates out of Central Islip and serves the communities of Point O' Woods, Ocean Beach Park, and Seaview. Steve Young primarily serves Davis Park. His fleet includes a cargo boat that can accommodate very heavy equipment, including a moving van, a concrete mixer, and a garbage truck.

Lateral Water Transport

Fire Island Ferries operate Fire Island Water Taxi, the only lateral water transport service on Fire Island. Officially, Fire Island Water Taxi runs between Fire Island Lighthouse and the Watch Hill Visitors Center, stopping at all communities with public dock facilities. The taxi service is run on-demand, seven days a week from Memorial Day through the weekend after Labor Day, with charter service available at other times. One-way ticket prices range from $6 to $22 for adults and $3 to $11 for children. Ferry operators anecdotally note that the water taxi does not currently serve Fire Island Lighthouse or Watch Hill Visitor Center and that the water taxi operator is reluctant to travel to eastern parts of the Island due to low profitability.

In the 1980s, market demand supported at least three water taxi companies offering lateral water transport service. In some cases, there were exclusive agreements between particular communities and companies to provide service. The companies had independent owners and operated smaller boats than does the current service. Most of the companies went out of business by the 1990s, leaving Fire Island Ferries as the only water taxi operator. Current ferry operators, who have witnessed the demise of several water taxi companies, note that current Fire Island residents and visitors do not demand lateral travel to the same degree they once did. The reasons cited include stricter DWI laws, a less raucous party atmosphere, and older and wealthier residents with less inclination to travel laterally on the Island.

The service now operated by Fire Island Ferries has the advantages of the company's infrastructure and maintenance capabilities. The Fire Island Water Taxi uses larger boats: bow loaders and large skiffs with inboard/outboard or outboard motors. The larger boats must travel further offshore to find adequately deep waters and use the deep channels into the communities' docks.

It is generally recognized that the lateral water transport market will not support more than one service. Late night demand for lateral taxi service is far below historic figures, including formerly busy weekend night routes, for example, between Cherry Grove and Fire Island Pines. The late night demand for regular ferry service has also fallen in recent years.

Recreational and Work Boats

Recreational boats

Privately-owned recreational boats are a significant sector of water-based transport on Fire Island, for both Island residents and visitors. With four marinas open to the public and 10 to 12 marinas operated by private communities, many use private boats both to travel to and recreate around Fire Island. Fire Island Concessions, under contract with NPS, operates a 42-slip marina at Sailors Haven and a 188-slip marina at Watch Hill, both with full facilities to accommodate overnight visitors. The small marina at Sailors Haven consistently is filled with boats and has high turnover rates, with additional boats mooring off-shore for day use and dropping off passengers at a specially-designed drop point dock. Watch Hill is usually less full on weekdays, though it fills on weekends. Boaters must pay for slips at Watch Hill in 24-hour increments, which discourages day use of the facility. Rates at both NPS marinas, at the time of the study (2009), are $1.75 per foot of boat per 24-hour period. Watch Hill day visitors tend to moor off-shore and drop passengers and cargo at one of many informal drop points. At Old Inlet, 20 slips are available for boaters. An NPS rule limits visitors to two weeks at the marinas, with a requirement to vacate the slip for 48 hours before returning.

The Town of Islip operates a public marina (over 150 slips) at Atlantique Beach that primarily serves Islip residents. Boats with an Islip resident decal are accepted on a first-come, first-served basis seven days a week. Non-residents may use the facility on weekdays (Monday through Thursday) or on slow weekends at the dockmaster's discretion. All users pay slip fees based on the width of the boat, and they are permitted to stay up to 12 consecutive days. The marina operates from May through Labor Day, and then weekends only in October. The Town of Brookhaven operates a marina in Davis Park (over 200 slips), which is open to both residents and non-residents on a first-come, first-served basis. Fees are based both on residency and size of vessel.

Additionally, several communities offer publicly-owned marinas, community- or privately-owned finger pier docks, or mooring space in the bay to accommodate residents and visitors traveling by private boat. Communities have varying regulations for use of marina or dock facilities; some docks operate on a first-come, first-served basis while others take reservations. Some docks are open to all users while others require a permit issued by the village or community. Most marina and dock facilities charge user fees, which may vary by size of boat, residency, and season.

Work boats

Many public and commercial entities own and operate their own boats on Fire Island. The public entities include the National Park Service and local law enforcement and emergency services agencies. The private entities include contractors and utilities. These boats are an important transport asset for Fire Island workers.

Work boats range from the fleet of boats used by NPS rangers to single vessels owned by private contractors. Some workers only use their boats during the summer, when driving is prohibited, whereas others use boats year-round. One challenge cited by almost all workers who use private boats was the difficulty in docking to access job sites, although some contractors have private arrangements or use of slips that allow them to dock their boats. In many cases, community docks do not maintain slips for these workers, especially during peak summer months. Many private employers cited lack of dock space as one of the key reasons they use vehicles instead of boats for on-Island work.

FIIS has its own fleet of boats, with certain boats assigned to NPS divisions and outfitted accordingly. For example, maintenance boats are better able to accommodate construction materials and supplies for repairs. NPS owns a barge that can transport vehicles to Fire Island. The boats are stored at a NPS maintenance facility, adjacent to the Patchogue ferry terminal. NPS employees have several advantages that allow them to travel more by water, one of which being their access to designated slips at NPS docking facilities (both on Fire Island and Long Island). NPS has no set system to coordinate cross-bay travel, and coordination is complicated by the fact that some employees live on Fire Island and some on Long Island, with different job site destinations. NPS also pays for ferry tickets for employees, most of whom commute to Watch Hill or Sailors Haven by ferry in season.

Other work boats include the following:

- Suffolk County Marine Bureau has a fleet of boats that patrol the Great South Bay, including waters around Fire Island. On a typical summer day, four to five boats cover the Great South Bay. SCMB also has water ambulances, used depending on conditions in the bay and the condition of the patient. SCMB also uses their patrol boats to take arrested persons off the Island. Suffolk County boats are stored at their Timber Point facility; no boats are stored on-Island.
- Other municipal and emergency service providers have personnel that use their own boats, though these boats are used with less regularity than the SCMB fleet. Some firefighters use boats to fight fires near the bay; these boats may be owned by towns, villages, or community volunteer fire districts. For example, Ocean Beach has an unofficial fire boat.

  Islip has two town boats used by lifeguards, two work boats used by a dock building crew, and three harbor police units that often patrol the waterways and communities from Ocean Bay Park west to the single-span bridge and all the islands north of Fire Island Shores.. Islip's lifeguard boats, which are used daily during the summer, are stored in Atlantique and not licensed to carry passengers. Islip's boat fleet is almost exclusively used in the summer.

Town of Brookhaven personnel from the Highway Department use two boats to travel to Fire Island regularly for boardwalk maintenance and repair. Brookhaven personnel from other departments reportedly travel to the Island by boat for tasks such as code inspection and response to complaints. However, some municipal staff report that personnel from several Brookhaven departments are more likely to drive in from Smith Point than to use boats for these tasks.[26]

- Long Island Power Authority (LIPA) is the only utility that operates a boat, a 21-foot vessel that is kept at the Ocean Beach marina. LIPA employees use the boat for lateral travel on Fire Island from April to November, especially during summer weekends when lateral vehicle travel is difficult. LIPA reports that their employees have not had problems with docking the boat during jobs, possibly due to the essential and short-term nature of their work. LIPA has maintained a boat on the Island for the past 40 years. The boat carries one or more field technicians and small equipment, such as tools and ladders. LIPA employees report that fueling the boat on Fire Island is not always feasible and that they occasionally make a special trip to the mainland to use the LIPA fueling facilities in Patchogue and Brentwood. Other utilities that do not have their own boats, such as the Suffolk County Water Authority, will ride on an Islip or Brookhaven town boat to access the Island in an emergency.

- Contractors, who form the largest employee user group on the Island, generally travel by vehicle rather than boat during the driving season (Appendix B shows specific 2010 driving dates for all user groups). During the summer season, contractors working in the eastern communities will either use the ferry service or their own private boats, which they keep in mainland marinas and "commute" across the Bay to work on Fire Island. Contractors working on the east end of the Island where vehicle access is more difficult are more likely to have private boats. Contractors report that owning these boats is more cost-effective for them than paying for ferry tickets and conforming to ferry schedules. Many of these contractors and their employees live in Patchogue or Sayville and travel to their job sites by private boat, often doing triangle runs to cover multiple sites per day. Contractor boat use on the western part of the Island does occur, but much less commonly, and these contractors face docking challenges.

Docks

Docks serve as transportation hubs for water- and land-based modes on Fire Island and are the primary entry point for people and goods. Docks and marinas accommodate passenger and freight ferries and private boats, as well as golf carts, UTVs, and other vehicles that come to retrieve goods and cargo. Community commercial areas, if they exist, are almost always located adjacent to the dock area. There are commonly storage areas for wagons (to transport personal belongings from ferries to residences), community information kiosks, and temporarily storage structures proximate to the docks.

While NPS owns and maintains all of the docks for the National Seashore sites, dock ownership varies in the other communities. In some cases the community owns and maintains its dock, financed by homeowner's association fees or taxes. In other cases, the Towns of Islip and Brookhaven own the docks. Islip owns all or part of the docks in Kismet and Atlantique Beach, and Brookhaven owns all or parts of the docks in Cherry Grove, Fire Island Pines, and Davis Park. Additionally, several of the ferry companies own the docks used by individual communities. In cases where the ferries do not own docks, they must make a formal agreement with the dock owner to operate ferries on the dock. Table 2 shows dock ownership for the docks in use on Fire Island, as well as other information about water-based transportation and Figures 7 and 8 depict important infrastructure and service features of the docks.

Dock capacity to handle freight and heavy equipment is an important consideration for the operations of Island businesses, the needs of homeowners, and the provision of utility services. While all docks can handle passenger transport and limited freight, several have the capacity to handle heavier or bulkier

---

[26] Town of Brookhaven officials outside the Highway Department did not respond to requests for interviews. This information is on the basis of interviews with FIIS personnel and other public and private service providers on Fire Island.

freight or specialized kinds of freight. The communities of Saltaire, Ocean Beach, Point O' Woods, and Fire Island Pines all have separate docks or separate areas of their marina to accommodate freight. This capability allows these docks to handle both food deliveries and garbage hauling, as New York state law prohibits garbage hauling to use the same facilities as food delivery. The docks at Saltaire, Ocean Beach, Cherry Grove and Fire Island Pines are capable of handling heavy equipment, including vehicles and construction equipment needed for major repairs on the Island. However, communities with capacity to handle heavy equipment have expressed reluctance or unwillingness to allow other communities to use their facilities. While Cherry Grove's dock can handle all kinds of freight, the lack of road infrastructure in the community limits the utility of the dock capability.

Many areas of Fire Island have a similar mismatch between dock capabilities and land-based infrastructure. For example, the Village of Saltaire recently completed renovations to its dock that allow it to offload vehicles and other heavy equipment. However, most walks in the Village cannot accommodate this equipment. Saltaire enhanced its dock capacity to meet its long-term goal of hauling garbage off the Island by barge, but this goal cannot be realized until Broadway (the main north-south walk) is restructured, which may be many years away. In Fire Island Pines, a separate dock area can accommodate very heavy equipment, including major propane tanks and large dumpsters, but the inland infrastructure consists of sand roads and pedestrian boardwalks. All heavy equipment brought to the Pines is confined to the dock area.

Table 2
Dock and Ferry Table
Source: NPS and Volpe Center

Community	Ferry Service	Seasonality of Ferry Service	Water Taxi Service	Dock Ownership	Freight (Dry)	Freight (Food)	Freight House	Vehicle Transport by Boat	Trash Hauling
Fire Island Lighthouse	No scheduled service. Dock used for NPS boats, private charter, and limited water taxi service	NA	Limited	NPS	Minimal	None	No	None	Garbage driven off island
Kismet	Fire Island Ferries	April to October	Yes	Finger pier owned by Kismet; wave curtain owned by Islip; passenger part of dock owned by Fire Island Ferries (FIF)	Fire Island Ferries; no separate freight dock	Fire Island Ferries	No	None	Garbage driven off island
Saltaire	Fire Island Ferries	Year-round, weather permitting	Yes	Saltaire; 5-10 year leasing agreement with FIF	Fire Island Ferries; no separate freight dock	Fire Island Ferries	Cartage concessionaire	Heavy equipment and vehicles - capable	Garbage driven off island, but may change to Fire Island Ferries
Fair Harbor	Fire Island Ferries	April to December	Yes	FIF owns a small pier with capacity for one ferry; community owns a second pier with 20-30 slips	Fire Island Ferries	Fire Island Ferries	Yes	None	Fire Island Ferries
Dunewood	Fire Island Ferries	April to October	Yes	Small, privately owned finger pier dock	Fire Island Ferries	Fire Island Ferries	No	None	Garbage driven off island
Lonelyville	No regular ferry service	NA	No	Privately owned	None	None	No	None	Garbage driven off island
Atlantique Beach	Fire Island Ferries	July to September, associated with summer camp	No	Islip	None	None	No	None	Garbage driven off island
Atlantique	Fire Island Ferries	May to September	Yes	Atlantique; 5-10 year leasing agreement with FIF	Fire Island Ferries	Fire Island Ferries	No	Fire Island Ferries	Garbage driven off island
Robbins Rest	No regular ferry service	NA	Yes	Privately owned dock	None	None	No	None	Garbage driven off island
Fire Island Summer Club	No regular ferry service	NA	No	?Privately owned dock	None	None	No	None	Garbage driven off island
Corneille Estates	No regular ferry service	NA	No	None	None	None	No	None	Garbage driven off island

Community	Ferry Service	Seasonality of Ferry Service	Water Taxi Service	Dock Ownership	Freight (Dry)	Freight (Food)	Freight House	Vehicle Transport	Trash Hauling
Ocean Beach	Fire Island Ferries	Year-round, weather permitting	Yes	Ocean Beach; 5-to year leasing agreement with FIF	Fire Island Ferries; separate dock	Fire Island Ferries	Yes	Fire Island Ferries	Fire Island Ferries and Tony's Barge
Seaview	Fire Island Ferries	April to October	Yes	Fire Island Ferries	Fire Island Ferries; comes by ramp	Fire Island Ferries	Yes	Golf carts come by cargo ferry; vehicle-capable	Tony's Barge; joint garbage district with Ocean Bay Park
Ocean Bay Park	Fire Island Ferries	April to November	Yes	Fire Island Ferries	Fire Island Ferries	Fire Island Ferries	Yes	Brookhaven barge	Tony's Barge
Point O'Woods	Private ferry (open to residents only)	NA	Yes	Point O'Woods corporation	Private or by charter (Fire Island Ferries); separate freight dock	Private or Fire Island Ferries (MV America) by charter	Owned by Corporation?	Fire Island Ferries (America) by charter	Fire Island Ferries or Tony's Barge
Sailors Haven	Sayville Ferry	May to October	Yes	NPS owns dock	NPS (Seahorse) and Sayville Ferry	NPS (workboat "Seahorse") and Sayville Ferry	NA	None	Tony's Barge
Cherry Grove	Sayville Ferry	Year-round, weekends only, weather permitting	Yes	Brookhaven	Sayville Ferry; most large freight delivered to freight dock at Fire Island Pines	Sayville Ferry; delivered to passenger dock	No	Town of Brookhaven barge	Tony's Barge
Fire Island Pines	Sayville Ferry	Year-round, weekends only, weather permitting	Yes	Brookhaven owns and maintains part of dock; private ownership of docks (including passenger dock) around commercial area	Sayville Ferry and Tony's Barge; separate freight dock area	Sayville Ferry	Cartage concessionaire	Town of Brookhaven barge	Tony's Barge
Water Island	Sayville Ferry	May to October	Yes	Water Island Community Association owns small dock	Sayville Ferry, but most freight comes into Fire Island Pines	Sayville Ferry	No	None	Tony's Barge (?)
Barrett Beach	None	NA	No	NPS	Dock used for unloading of NPS supplies	None	NA	None	None
Davis Park	Davis Park Ferry	March to November (limited service in Mar, Apr, Oct, and Nov)	Yes	Brookhaven	Davis Park Ferry	Davis Park Ferry	No	Town of Brookhaven	Tony's Barge
Watch Hill	Davis Park Ferry	May to October	Yes	NPS owns dock and marina	NPS (Seahorse) and Davis Park Ferry	NPS (Seahorse) and Davis Park Ferry	NA	None	NPS

Community	Ferry Service	Seasonality of Ferry Service	Water Taxi Service	Dock Ownership	Freight (Dry)	Freight (Food)	Freight House	Vehicle Transport	Trash Hauling
Bellport Beach	Private ferry (open to Village of Bellport residents)	May to September	No	Village of Bellport owns dock and marina	Private ferry for small concession deliveries	Private ferry	NA	Unknown	Unknown

Figure 7
Docks West: Lighthouse to Sailors Haven
Source: Volpe Center

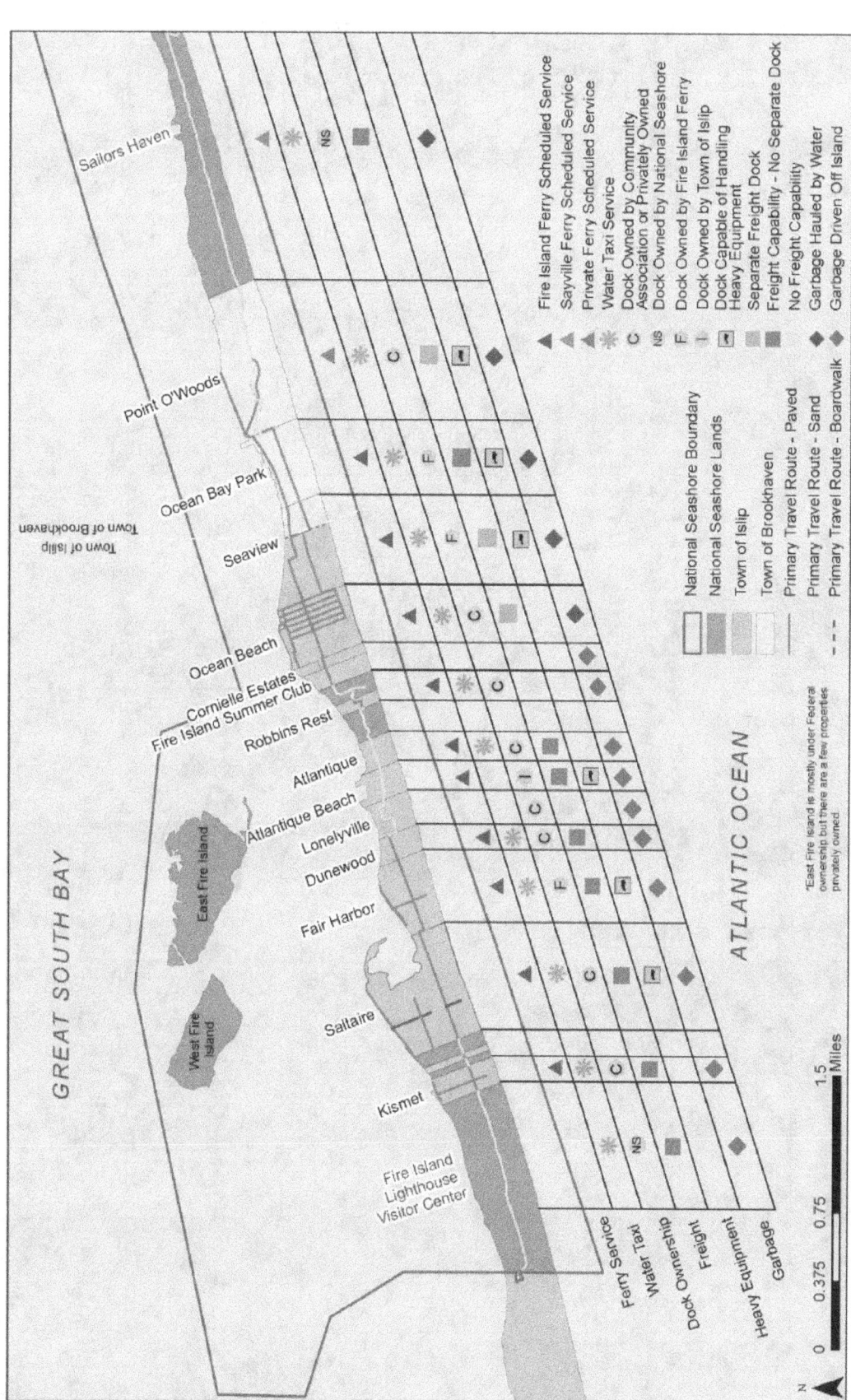

Figure 8
Docks East: Cherry Grove to Bellport Beach
Source: Volpe Center

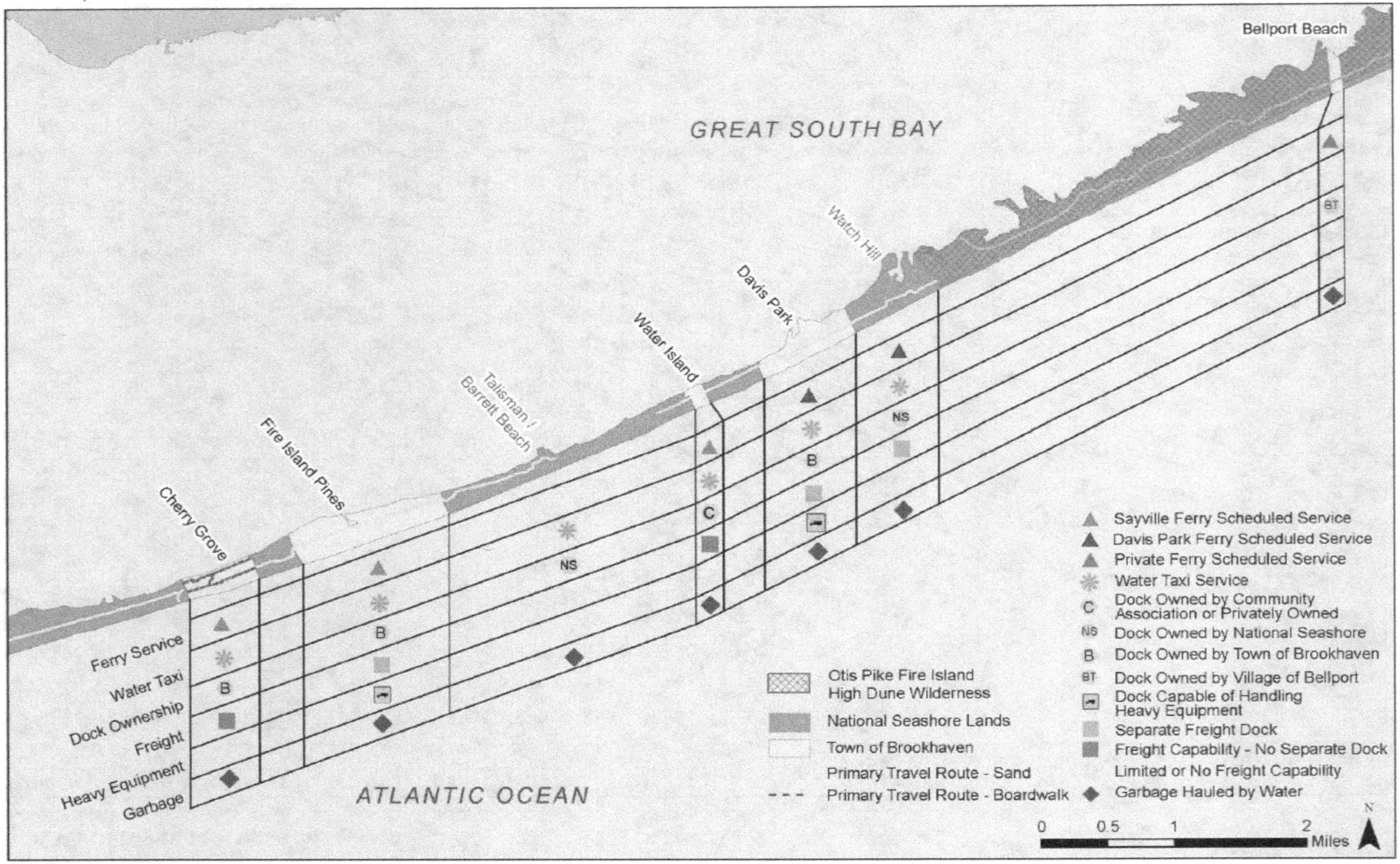

Conclusions / Observations

The marine transport services and dock and marina infrastructure provide for most transportation to and from Fire Island to go by water, particularly in the summertime. All major destinations on Fire Island have docks that can accommodate passenger and freight transport, while smaller communities or NPS sites have dock infrastructure sufficient to meet their needs or work cooperatively with neighboring communities to transport people and goods. Some users note that dock improvements, marina expansions, or new management policies would enhance the current system, but in most cases the infrastructure can support existing levels of use. A limitation exists in the intermodal transfer of passengers and materials once on Fire Island. Many communities in Fire Island do not have infrastructure to transport freight through the community. Even in communities that can accommodate vehicles, freight must often be transferred to a small truck or UTV to reach its final destination.

The ferry and freight operators have generally been responsive about meeting the needs of all their customers during different seasons. Their schedules during the summer months are capable of moving thousands of people across the Great South Bay and carting freight of all shapes and sizes. In some cases, schedules have changed over the past decade based on shifting customer demand, occasionally to the dissatisfaction of some passengers, but the total number and capacity of ferry runs is sufficient to meet most passengers' needs during the summer season. Off-season demand for ferry service drops off significantly and the users that remain dependent on the ferries have very limited transportation options. Many people who live or do business on Fire Island find it too inconvenient or expensive to adjust their schedules to the ferry schedules, or they find that they simply must depend on vehicles rather than ferries during the winter months.

Altogether the water transport options may present a viable alternative to vehicular transport, especially in the eastern communities where vehicle access is more challenging and during the off season when ferries are not available (for example, through increased use of private boats). The added expense and time of transporting materials by boat is more apparent in western communities, where driving on and off the Island is relatively more efficient (though actual times vary by destination, season, time of day, and conditions). Another important constraint is the politically-fragmented nature of the Fire Island communities and the lack of cooperation in matters of transportation. Opportunities for optimizing movements of freight, garbage, etc. and reducing vehicle use, keyed to the use of existing freight docks, are lost because of restrictions on movements among some of the communities.

Section 5 describes the vehicular use patterns on Fire Island, including those of users who chose to drive instead of using water-based transportation and those driving routes that are necessary to sustain basic Island operations.

Section 5: Vehicular Use Patterns

Introduction

While water-based transport may be the principal means of transporting people and goods to Fire Island, the services required to support the large population of residents and visitors necessitate some degree of vehicular driving on the Island. Vehicular use varies widely from the western communities, where driving to Long Island is relatively easy and efficient, to the eastern communities, where driving to the mainland is often much slower than boating. In many cases, systems of delivering goods and services have been established around the ease of driving in the western communities. Businesses operating in these communities discuss the need to use vehicles to remain economically competitive. In the eastern communities, water-based transport is built into the cost of doing business.

The vehicular travel patterns of user groups indicate that a variety of reasons compel drivers to use vehicles instead of water-based transport options. These reasons include sparse ferry service, length of travel, efficiency of transferring materials, need to haul specialized equipment, expense, and feasibility of completing specific tasks. This section describes vehicular use patterns by user group, including types of driving, transport of people and cargo, seasonality of travel, geographic range, and storage of vehicles.

Negotiated Rulemaking

The long-standing conflict between protecting the cultural and natural resources on Fire Island and providing services for residents and visitors has resulted in a complex set of rules governing driving on the Island. In an effort to reduce these conflicts and improve vehicular use regulations, NPS engaged consultants to conduct a year-long consensus-based negotiation process between 2002 and 2003. The regulatory negotiation culminated in the drafting of a Final Consensus Agreement that covered most, but not all, contentious issues. Participants in the negotiation included NPS, residents (seasonal and year-round), contractors, law enforcement personnel, ferry companies, municipalities, utilities, and environmental and conservation organizations.

The Final Consensus Agreement of the negotiation establishes the types and numbers of driving permits to be issued, when and where driving is permitted, and how the Island's natural resources will be protected from vehicular impacts. The Agreement also covers law enforcement driving, management and enforcement of driving, parking, transfer of driving permits, and exceptions to the rules. Driving permits are available to a limited number of year-round residents, a limited number of contractors, and a very limited number of seasonal residents. NPS grants fleet permits to the water, phone, and electric utilities; essential service permits for garbage haulers, plumbers, and electricians; and municipal permits to municipal or community employees. NPS also can grant special permits on a case-by-case basis for temporary uses, such as access to the Island during ice-over conditions when ferry service is suspended. The Agreement requires that contractors and essential services permit holders cannot haul building materials onto the Island; they must send these materials by ferry. A copy of the Final Consensus Agreement is available in Appendix A. Permitted driving dates differ by type of permit holder. A list of permitted driving dates for 2010 can be found in Appendix B. The formal regulations to implement the Agreement are still being finalized by NPS leadership.[27]

Driving regulations and permit use are enforced by NPS rangers.[28] Rangers are unable to enforce the regulations as closely as they would like, primarily due to budget constraints and rangers' limited patrol hours. Some rangers express a desire to have Suffolk County Police help with permit enforcement, especially during evening shifts. Despite some challenges with enforcement, rangers report that the vast majority of people abide by the regulations.

---

[27] Both Islip and Brookhaven have driving regulations included in their Town codes, but these regulations do not conform with those resulting from the negotiated rulemaking. Officials from both Towns assure that they will change their Town codes to conform with NPS regulations once the new driving regulations are finalized.

[28] The Suffolk County Police Department Marine Bureau can also enforce Town driving regulations but does not consider this a high priority function.

Vehicular Entrance Points to FIIS

Vehicles entering FIIS must pass through a checkpoint monitored by NPS. The main vehicular checkpoint is located near the Fire Island Lighthouse Visitor Center. The roads at Robert Moses State Park are paved, and the pavement ends at the FIIS boundary, where a sign notes that vehicles must have a Federal permit. At this point, the road turns to a crushed shell and gravel surface and continues for approximately one-half mile to the checkpoint gate and parking lot. Vehicular access to the lighthouse occurs along this one-half mile stretch, prior to the checkpoint gate, such that vehicles can drop off passengers at the lighthouse. While there is limited parking at the lighthouse for handicapped visitors and staff, almost all lighthouse visitors park at Field 5 and walk along boardwalks. At the checkpoint gate, Federal permit holders can either use an electronic key or punch in a numeric code to open the gate. There is no person physically monitoring the gate. From the gate, vehicles must travel approximately one-half mile on a sand road to reach the community of Kismet. Road users report that this access road is often in poor driving condition.

Vehicles may also enter the Seashore through a checkpoint by the Wilderness Visitor Center, which offers beach vehicle access adjacent to the Otis Pike High Dune Wilderness area. The checkpoint does not have a gate, and is used far less than the one at the Lighthouse Visitor Center. The Wilderness Visitor Center checkpoint is used most by recreational permit holders (including hunters and fishers), and these permits are issued at the Visitor Center. Recreational permit holders must enter before 9 a.m. or after 6 p.m. The Visitor Center has very little parking, limited to NPS vehicles only. All visitors, including those who wish to purchase a recreational permit, must park at the Smith Point parking field and walk. The Wilderness Visitor Center entrance is also used by contractors and other workers with job sites in the eastern communities.

A third, less common means for vehicles to enter the Seashore is by barge. Several barges (described in Section 4) are equipped to transport vehicles, and a few communities have docks and road infrastructure capable of handling heavier vehicles and equipment. Generally, vehicle transport by water is only used with very heavy vehicles that cannot travel across the Robert Moses Causeway due to weight limitations or that would not be able to travel on the Island's sand routes. Garbage vehicles and some construction vehicles occasionally travel by barge to a community in Fire Island (where they must stay within the community because they lack a permit to cross into Federal lands), and this practice is more common in the eastern communities.

Vehicular Patterns of User Groups

The specific needs and travel patterns of individual permitted drivers within each of the many Fire Island user groups dictate their travel patterns. Even within one user group, travel patterns may vary by geographic location, seasonality, time of day, cargo, number of passengers, and type of vehicle. While recognizing that drivers within each user group may have a diversity of needs, NPS issues permits by general category of user groups, with several use trends apparent within these groups, though shared patterns emerge between groups. In particular, employees of utilities, municipalities, and contractors tend to do similar kinds of work in terms of construction, repair, and maintenance. They also tend to concentrate their work into the shoulder or off-seasons, wherever possible. Through a detailed description of the specific travel patterns of the user groups, opportunities and conflicts emerge.

Figure 9 depicts a schematic map of user groups, including the size of vehicle fleet, geographic range, and locations of key activities. Information on the Map has been approximated from interview responses to offer a picture of how different user groups travel laterally around the Island and where hubs of activity are likely to occur. As seasonality plays a key role in Fire Island's vehicular patterns, Figure 10 shows Seasonality and Intensity of Vehicular Use by user group. This graphic offers a complement to the geographic range of use by illustrating the activity of selected user groups by season. Darker shading represents higher relative intensity of vehicular travel within a user group. For example, Suffolk County Water Authority travels to all pump stations on Fire Island at least once a day during the summer, making this their most intense period of activity, while their winter pump maintenance is less frequent. Figure 10 is also based on interview responses from representatives of each user group.

Figure 9
Schematic Map of User Groups
Source: Volpe Center

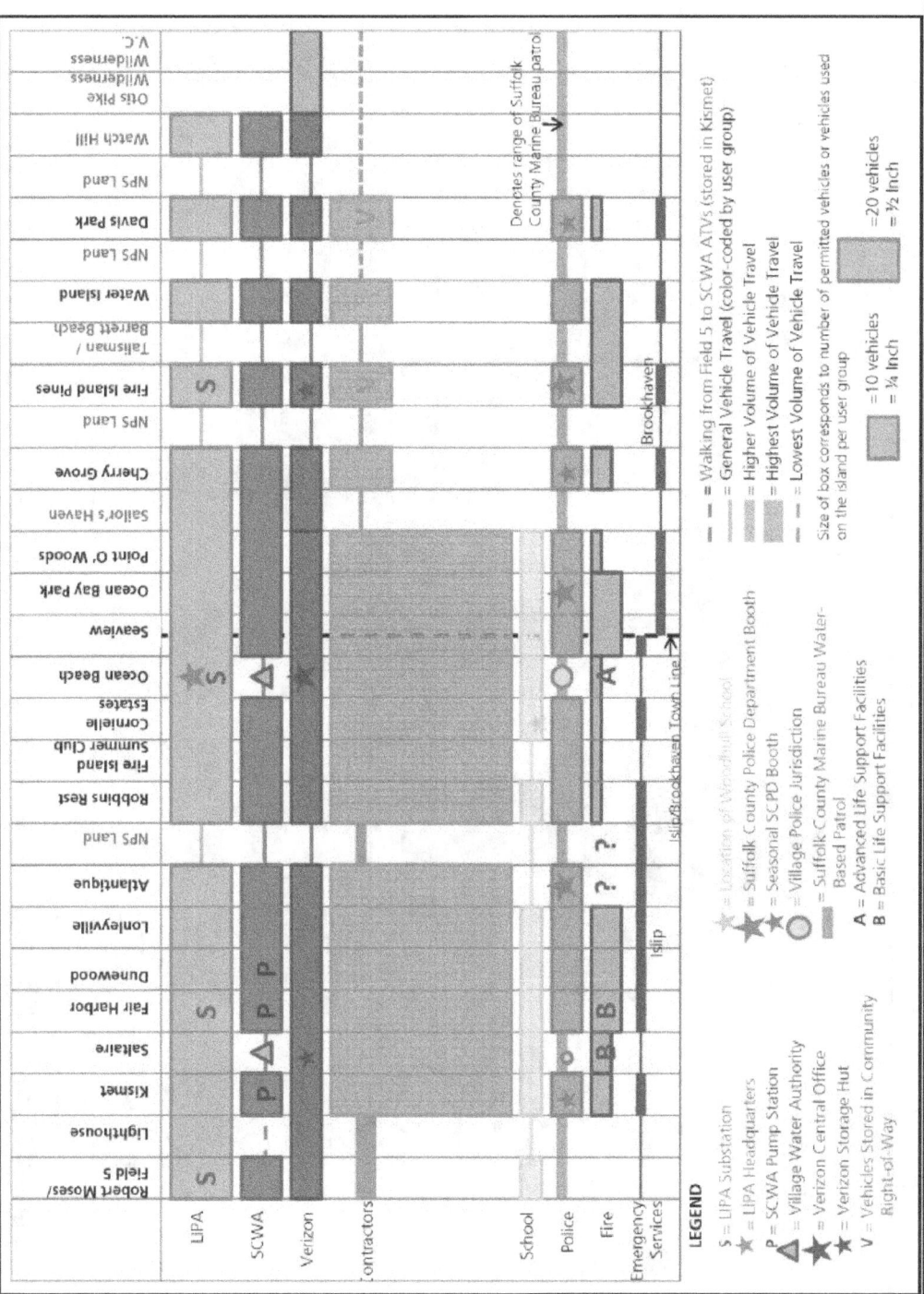

Note: The data represents current conditions. The bus route services communities based on existing student populations.

Figure 10
Seasonality and Intensity of Vehicular Use
Source: Volpe Center

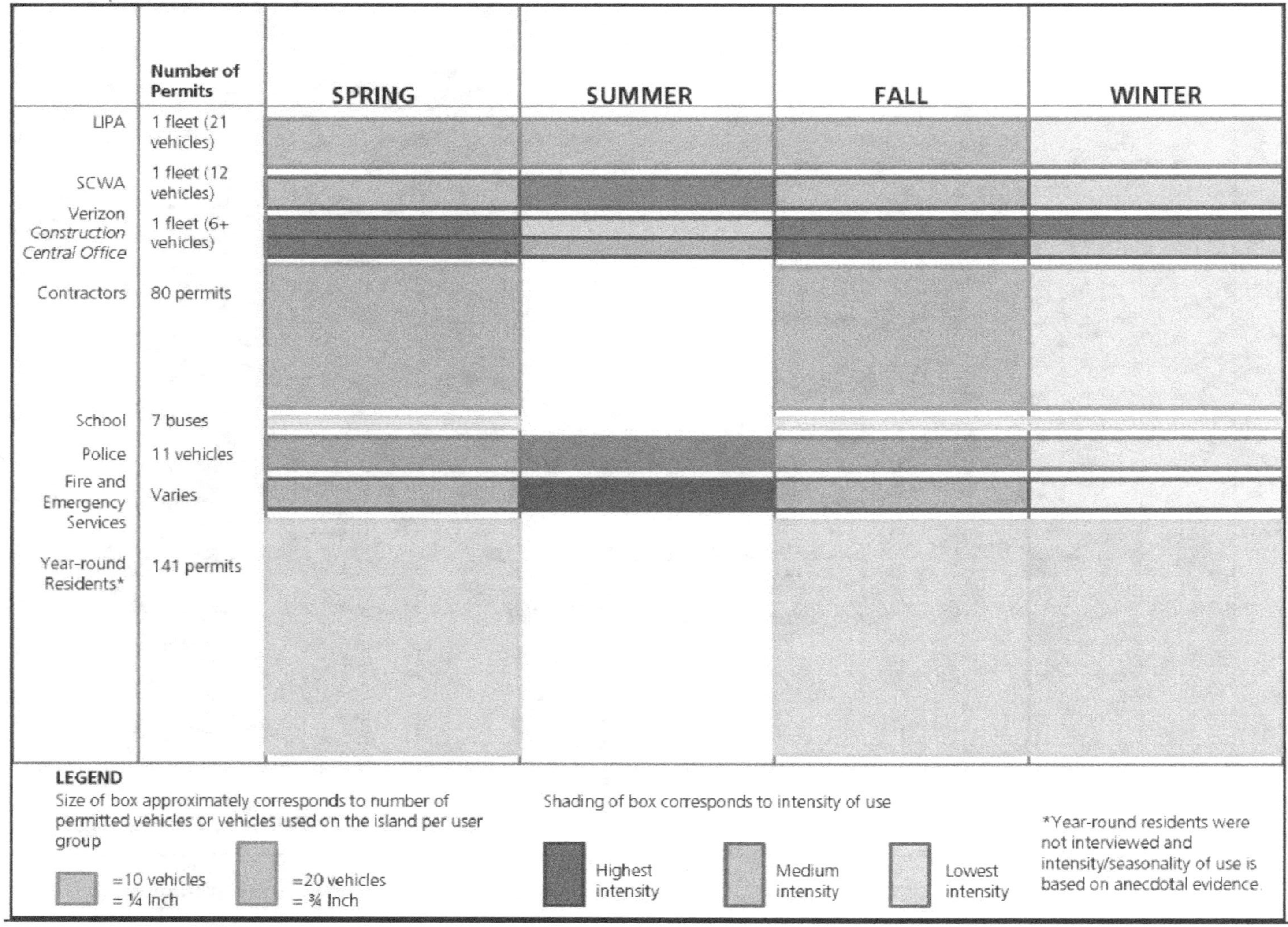

	Number of Permits	SPRING	SUMMER	FALL	WINTER
LIPA	1 fleet (21 vehicles)				
SCWA	1 fleet (12 vehicles)				
Verizon Construction Central Office	1 fleet (6+ vehicles)				
Contractors	80 permits				
School	7 buses				
Police	11 vehicles				
Fire and Emergency Services	Varies				
Year-round Residents*	141 permits				

LEGEND

Size of box approximately corresponds to number of permitted vehicles or vehicles used on the island per user group

▪ = 10 vehicles / = ¼ Inch
▪ = 20 vehicles / = ¾ Inch

Shading of box corresponds to intensity of use

Highest intensity | Medium intensity | Lowest intensity

*Year-round residents were not interviewed and intensity/seasonality of use is based on anecdotal evidence.

Fire Island National Seashore Alternative Transportation Study

Utilities

The three permitted utilities operating on Fire Island are the Suffolk County Water Authority (SCWA), Verizon, and the Long Island Power Authority (LIPA). Each of the utilities has a fleet permit, which entitles the bearer to have multiple permitted vehicles under one permit. Fleet permits are issued for two years, unlike other permits which must be renewed on an annual basis.

SCWA is a not for profit, state chartered, public benefit corporation that exists solely to supply water to its customers. The SCWA service area on Fire Island extends from Kismet to Davis Park/Watch Hill (with the exception of Saltaire, Ocean Beach, and Seaview). SCWA delivers water both for public consumption and for fire protection. SCWA has twelve vehicles in its fleet and three Polaris "4-wheelers" to perform daily maintenance at pump stations located in most communities across the Island. The Water Authority's responsibilities include maintaining and operating pump stations, overseeing the distribution system and customer connections, repairing large water mains, and emergency work. The infrastructure, namely the wells and pump stations, require routine daily servicing and, when necessary, rapid emergency response. SCWA's permitted vehicles are mostly pick-up trucks with a few larger trucks for main repairs, and they are used regularly during the winter for maintenance and in the summer for emergency pipeline repairs. The Water Authority, perhaps more than any other user group, has made efforts to use smaller vehicles (the Polaris vehicles) to meet frequent travel needs during the summer months; these vehicles are less intrusive than full-size pick-up trucks. Some types of repairs require the use of a full size 4WD vehicles.

SCWA has two pump station operators that laterally traverse the Island daily in Polarises to treat pumps and collect samples. The pump operators generally park their vehicles at Field 5 and walk to the Kismet pump station, where the Polarises are stored. The only community that cannot be accessed by Polaris is Cherry Grove, which must be served by foot from the beach. Pumps must be serviced during the summer to supply water treatment chemicals, and on a daily basis because of the tanks' small storage volumes. In the winter, some pump stations are serviced daily and others less frequently. Chemicals are transported by ferries and stocked as much as possible in pump stations. Kismet is used as a base to store the bulk of chemicals, which are transported to Kismet by truck in the spring. Two additional field employees in the beach pipeline division travel to the repair site by vehicle or by ferry, depending on the location of the repair and the availability of ferry service. The pipeline trucks are used regularly all winter for maintenance and on an emergency basis during the summer; they are stored on Long Island.

Verizon and LIPA both have several departments operating on Fire Island, with distinct responsibilities within the realm of providing phone and electric service, respectively. While departments within each utility try to work cooperatively to minimize duplicative trips, each departments has unique service needs and equipment. Transportation patterns therefore differ even within one utility.

Verizon maintains a fleet of approximately eight vehicles working in three departments on the Island: Central Office, Construction, and Installation and Repair. The Central Office (CO) manages the equipment that allows customers to make calls and the computers where calls are generated. They provide dial tones, add new service, add new DSL, maintain existing service, and maintain circuits. The CO Department employs one person, full-time, from May through September, who works at an office in Ocean Beach and commutes by ferry. From October through April, CO employees only travel to Fire Island once or twice per week; travel is by vehicle because their short trips are not compatible with ferry schedules. CO employees can temporarily park vehicles at the Ocean Beach office, but they do not leave the department vehicles there overnight. The department responds to emergencies 24 hours a day, which may necessitate a vehicle trip to Fire Island from the mainland.

The Construction Department is responsible for poles, cables, and connections to customer houses. Their work requires heavy equipment, and they regularly use four-wheel-drive vehicles, which are stored in Fire Island Pines and the Central Office in Ocean Beach. The department's four full-time employees generally drive to get to the Island during the off-season, although they will occasionally take the ferry in the summer if it is compatible with their schedule. This department uses vehicles for lateral transport year-round. Generally a truck will be driven back to Long Island once a week, even during the summer, to restock supplies in the two storage huts. The Construction Department operates in two zones: Sunken Forest to Davis Park, with supplies stored in a hut in the Pines, and Kismet to Point O' Woods, with supplies stored in a hut in Ocean Beach. Some large equipment and cables are barged to the Island because they are too heavy to drive across sand. These are then carried by hand or pick-up truck to the job site. Damaged poles and cables are cut into small pieces and driven off the Island.

The Installation and Repair Department installs new lines, jacks, and outside extensions. Their nine employees work in three zones: Kismet to Fair Harbor, Dunewood to Point O' Woods, and Cherry Grove to Davis Park. In addition to the storage huts in Fire Island Pines and Point O' Woods, Verizon rents a shed from Saltaire Fire Department for storage and electrical and phone access. Most work is concentrated in the off-season, although the Department responds to emergency repairs during the summer. While vehicles are used during the off-season, the Department uses bicycles for on-Island transport during the summer.

LIPA has 21 vehicles within five separate divisions working on the Island. LIPA owns all electrical equipment on the Island and contracts with National Grid for employees; all employees working for LIPA on the Island are National Grid employees. An important part of LIPA's work is emergency response, and to help meet that capacity, LIPA has one employee living on the Island and maintains a large vehicle fleet to transport other employees.

The System Operations Department is responsible for load switching or emergency switching. They have a full-time employee living in Ocean Beach in a house owned by LIPA. A truck, a Polaris, and a bicycle are stored at this house, and the employee can use any of these or the aforementioned LIPA boat to travel laterally around the Island. If the resident employee needs assistance with emergency response, additional employees will travel to the Island by vehicle or ferry, depending on ferry availability.

The Overhead and Underground Department is responsible for general maintenance and wire replacement. An average of four employees, traveling in two vehicles, are on the beach daily during the spring, summer, and fall, and these employees will travel laterally by truck to any part of the Island that needs service. Maintenance trips are on an as-needed basis in the winter.

The Meter Department does meter readings and replacements as well as cut-ons and cut-offs. The department has one vehicle, based in Patchogue, that works on the east end of the Island (Fire Island Pines and points east) and one vehicle, based in Brentwood, that works on the west end (Cherry Grove and points west). Meter readings must occur year-round, and they try to use automatic readings when possible. Employees travel to the Island less frequently than other departments and try to coordinate rides with other LIPA departments, when possible.

The Substation Maintenance Department and the Security Department both travel to Fire Island on an occasional basis, only for specific jobs. Substation Maintenance completes large substation overhauls in which three to four employees travel to the job site, often with specialized heavy equipment. Security travels to the Island once a year to check substation security and fencing; they travel by ferry and Polaris.

While some LIPA departments do make efforts to coordinate vehicle trips, employees cite several complications with inter-departmental coordination. Emergency response jobs cannot be predicted in advance, so these employees must be independently mobile. Departments use different types of equipment, which they store in their vehicles, making the sharing of vehicles difficult. Also, employees note differences in their schedules and location of jobs sites. Nonetheless, compared to other user groups, LIPA is able to minimize trips related to carting materials as they can stockpile materials at any of their four substations (located at Robert Moses State Park, Fair Harbor, Ocean Beach, and Fire Island Pines). They can also bring extra materials onto the Island in advance of a storm or if they anticipate that travel will otherwise be interrupted. They currently use their own pick-up trucks or local garbage haulers to drive off debris from construction and maintenance jobs.

Employees also note that LIPA company policies dictate the types of vehicles they can purchase, including restrictions on four-wheel drive vehicles. The company-wide trend towards smaller and hybrid vehicles is incompatible with ease of travel on Fire Island.

Essential Services

Essential service permits are granted for electricians and plumbers, who have individual driving permits, and for companies that transport fuel, gas, and refuse. The latter group of propane and solid waste carters are granted fleet permits. All essential permit holders may drive year-round, although they must abide by seasonally restricted driving hours and locations. Most essential services vehicles are stored off-Island, although some vehicles are left in the right-of-way in Fire Island Pines and in Davis Park.

Propane and gas are delivered to the eastern communities by barge, with the major entry point at the Fire Island Pines freight dock. An essential services contractor meets the freight barge with a vehicle to deliver propane to users. A new policy to reduce driving trips has resulted in the transport of larger propane tanks that can be delivered less frequently. Several year-round residents noted that these larger tanks pose a potential safety hazard, as they cannot be moved by emergency personnel in the event of a fire.

Image 2
Propane Delivery at Fire Island Pines
Source: Volpe Center

Garbage on Fire Island is removed by barge or by vehicle, depending on the location of the community. Ocean Beach and all communities to the east haul their garbage by barge (mostly by Tony's Barge), while the western communities have municipal solid waste agreements with land-based hauling services. As an added logistical challenge for vehicle-based hauling, regulations limit the hours that essential permit holders can drive during summer months. From June 15 to September 15, essential services permitted vehicles may only drive through NPS lands before 9 a.m. or after 6 p.m. Garbage vehicles are also restricted from the beach when piping plovers are present, requiring trucks to drive through communities early in the morning.

Tony's Barge, the principal land-based hauler for the western communities, has a fleet of approximately five vehicles that make up to three trips daily in the summer to collect municipal garbage. The number of daily trips decreases to approximately two in the shoulder season and as little as one trip per week during the winter season. For the water-based hauling, pick-up trucks or UTVs retrieve solid waste from residences and deliver the waste to the barge. Ocean Beach has a full-size garbage truck that travels only a few hundred feet from its dock and acts as a compactor; it is hauled off by barge.

Most community docks are not equipped to handle garbage transfer by barge. While unloading an empty dumpster onto the bay front is relatively easy, specialized equipment would be required to move a dumpster filled with garbage back onto the barge. Also, garbage and debris has to be transferred to the dock by vehicle, usually either a pick-up truck or an UTV, then transferred to the boat, then transferred back to a vehicle once on Long Island. Each transfer adds time, difficulty, and cost to the process. Other challenges with water-based hauling lie in residents' resistance to storing dumpsters in their communities and resistance to the added expense.

Based on these challenges, the removal of debris from the Island is generally done by vehicle. The nature of construction debris makes it very difficult to transfer between multiple travel modes. Many users expressed that once they load debris into their truck to transfer it to a cargo ferry, they might as well just drive it off and avoid extra transfers and expense. Contractors almost always haul debris by vehicle, even though they are required to bring construction materials to the Island by freight ferry. Community and municipal employees, contractors, utilities, and other workers try to minimize large construction or repair jobs during summer months, when hauling debris would be most disruptive. Many repairs are done on an emergency basis only.

Municipal

Municipalities on Fire Island (the Towns of Brookhaven and Islip and the Villages of Saltaire and Ocean Beach) may use municipal driving permits to drive on the Island year-round. Communities may also apply for these permits, with no more than five permits per community or municipality and no more than 30 municipal permits total.

The Town of Islip contracts all of its concrete road maintenance to subcontractors, who drive onto the Island with their equipment and employees. Road repairs are concentrated in late fall and early winter, to avoid conflicts with home repairs in the spring. Due to the heavy equipment needed to demolish concrete and to move debris and materials, Islip personnel believe that these jobs would be too costly to do by boat. The Islip Parks Department completes scheduled boardwalk repairs during the off-season, with town vehicles driving in materials and driving out rubble. Town trucks are also used for emergency repairs, which occur frequently (minor repairs are often handled by the community).

While Brookhaven owns several boats that make regular work trips to Fire Island, many employees and materials also travel by vehicle. The Brookhaven Highway Department usually drives one or more trucks onto the Island to meet its barge and complete repair jobs. Trucks are a key means of transporting most of the 10 Department employees who work daily on Fire Island. During winter months, Brookhaven relies more heavily on trucks to carry materials and workers to Fire Island, whereas more employees and supplies travel by boat in the summer.

Ocean Beach does small repair jobs for its concrete walks, bringing over concrete mix by ferry and transferring rubble to a village-owned truck that makes regular trips off the Island. The village truck then returns with sand from Long Island to mix with the concrete. Although Saltaire brings materials for boardwalk repair across the bay by barge, construction debris is removed by the village carter by driving. Saltaire hired a contractor to repair a 75 foot section of concrete walkway in November 2008. The job site was on the bay front, and therefore all work was done by barge. They are considering doing their next concrete walkway replacement by boat as well, but they face greater challenges as the site is not bay-front. Saltaire has one public works vehicle that leaves the beach daily carrying the water superintendent and three to four employees.

Contractors

The 80 contractors with driving permits highly value their ability to use their trucks on a daily basis, but they understand that driving regulations are based on a balance of competing interests. Contractors express support for driving restrictions in the summer, and in exchange they emphasize their need to drive during the rest of the year. Like other transportation operations on Fire Island, contractor travel needs and patterns vary between eastern and western communities. Contractors with driving permits also call for greater enforcement so that contractors as a whole are not blamed for violations of a few drivers.

Storage of materials and equipment is one of the greatest logistical challenges for contractors. Materials have to be brought in from Long Island on a daily basis because there is no place to store them on the job site or in communities. The Town of Islip prohibits storage of vehicles in the right-of-way, so contractors working in the western communities drive off daily. No such regulation exists in Brookhaven, and many contractors store golf carts or vehicles in the right-of-way in Fire Island Pines and Davis Park.

The transfer of freight (including materials and equipment) on and off the Island is the key motivation for contractor driving. Contractors use freight boats whenever possible; they simply cannot facilitate the enormous volume of customer freight with their own trucks. They also abide by regulations that require them to use ferry freight for the transfer of building materials, but contractors still drive trucks onto the Island to transfer materials from the ferry dock to the job site and to haul debris off the Island. In many cases, golf carts are not strong enough to transfer materials from ferries to job sites, and furthermore there would be nowhere on-Island to store the cart. Contractors also use trucks to carry certain types of freight, such as delicate landscaping materials or fragile cargo. While contractors do generally trust freight companies, ferries add additional exposure to the elements and the contractors feel they have more control over these fragile items by driving them. Many contractors also point out the inefficiencies with driving an empty truck onto the Island to meet the freight ferry when they could haul the materials by truck in the first place. Other situations cited in which vehicles are needed for hauling freight include an emergency job, cargo accidentally left on Long Island, a shipment that missed the ferry, and the transfer of materials that are prohibitively expensive to transfer by ferry (including sand, firewood, and stone).

While many contractors do have vehicle permits, these vehicles are not the primary means by which most contractor employees travel to Fire Island. Nearly all contractor employees that work east of Lonelyville travel by ferry; they generally take the 7 a.m. and 4:45 p.m. ferries during the off season and the shoulder season. When the bay freezes or when ferry service is suspended between December 10 and March 15, these workers travel by truck to the extent possible. Contractor employees working west of Lonelyville are often given the option of paid ferry tickets or a parking pass for Field 5. Almost all employees chose to park at Field 5 and bike to their job site because it saves time.

Contractors cited several additional challenges related to vehicular use patterns on Fire Island and related driving regulations. Some contractors expressed conflicts with Island residents, who complain about seeing trucks on the Island but also demand services that require vehicle use. Contractors believe that driving regulations are in response to resident complaints. Contractors also emphasize that they operate as small businesses, with limited flexibility and business models built around maximizing efficiency of transport. Many contractors expressed that their vehicles are essential to their operations, and any changes to driving regulations could mean costly changes to their business patterns.

Emergency Services

Throughout the multiple jurisdictions on Fire Island, a number of full-time and volunteer personnel meet the emergency service needs of communities and NPS areas. Emergency services include volunteer fire departments, law enforcement, EMS services, other medical treatment, and emergency management (including evacuations or other large-scale incidents). Representatives from each of the agencies providing emergency services on Fire Island serve on the Fire Island Law Enforcement and Safety Council. The Council was established to coordinate emergency response, law enforcement, and EMS services on the Island. Members of the Council maintain close communication and meet regularly to support each other in emergency and non-emergency situations.

Responders on Fire Island employ both an on-Island radio communication system and the County-wide mutual aid frequency to report the incident and get personnel to the scene. Communication is constantly monitored and addressed by law enforcement personnel, but it remains one of the greatest challenges in emergency services.

In the event of a medical emergency, a patient is treated by the first responder to the scene, who may be a volunteer firefighter, a Suffolk County police officer/EMT, a NPS Park Ranger/EMT, or a village or community doctor or medic in residence. Based on the patient's condition, he or she may be treated on the Island or evacuated to Long Island by boat, helicopter, or vehicle. For patients who are transported from the Island by boat, at least three agencies are involved in her care and transfer. First, the first responder treats and stabilizes the patient. Second, a Suffolk County police officer/EMT, Park Ranger, or medic treats the patient while she is on the Suffolk County Marine Bureau water ambulance. The water ambulance brings the patient to the SCPD Timber Point facility, located between West Sayville and East Islip, where she is transferred to a Town of Islip ambulance to drive to the hospital. Islip also has a water ambulance and rescue service; it is only used when the bay is calm enough to ensure safe transport.

Generally western communities can be served by vehicular ambulances; there are three such services serving Point O' Woods and points west. However, due to poor road conditions and crowded walks and beaches, vehicular travel may be problematic for patients. In the Town of Brookhaven, most ambulatory services must be done by water. If necessary, driving in restricted areas, such as along the beach or through the Wilderness, is permitted for extreme emergency situations.

Helicopters are used more generously on Fire Island than they would be on the mainland. Helicopters are used for life-threatening situations, such as cardiac arrest, CPR, and major lacerations, but they are also used in situations of patient comfort. If a patient has a painful injury, such as broken bones or dislocated joints, such that transport over sand roads by vehicle or over choppy bay waters would be very uncomfortable, a helicopter evacuation may be used. The cost is paid by Suffolk County taxpayers through the Police Department's Aviation Unit. While formal helicopter pads are located in Sailors Haven, Fire Island Pines, Davis Park, and Watch Hill, ballfields at Ocean Beach, Point O' Woods, and other locations may also be used as landing pads.

Emergency services rely on the cross-bay ferry companies to transport personnel to the Island for assistance in emergencies. The Fire Island Law Enforcement and Safety Council collaborate with all three ferry companies to provide these services, free of charge, in the event of emergency. As all the equipment is already stored on Fire Island, ferries are the fastest and most efficient way to get emergency personnel to the scene of the incident. Along with their agreements to assist in individual emergency incidents, the ferry companies also work cooperatively with emergency services personnel to plan for large-scale emergencies, such as evacuations or major fires. An emergency ferry schedule is in place to evacuate the Island in case of a major emergency. Other water-based enterprises (e.g. Tony's Barge Service) have also been engaged for emergency situations.

Fires are the biggest threat to public safety on Fire Island, due to the predominance of wood buildings and vegetation. Firefighting equipment unique to Fire Island is maintained by eight volunteer fire departments,[29] as the mainland trucks are not equipped to fight fires on the Island. Local volunteer firefighters are trained to bring the needed equipment to the scene of the incident and operate it appropriately. In these cases, other emergency services may coordinate to bring additional personnel – from other parts of Fire Island or from the mainland – to provide manpower to fight the fire.

Emergency services personnel maintain law enforcement patrols on the Island, employing a variety of modes including UTVs, sports utility vehicles, bike patrols, and foot patrols. Most vehicles are kept on the Island and equipped with rescue and medical supplies. Members of the Fire Island Law Enforcement Safety Council share resources and maintain cooperative agreements to minimize vehicular travel, especially during the summer season. For example, NPS provides Suffolk County police vehicles with gas so that they do not have to make off-Island trips for refueling (the County then reimburses the fuel to NPS at the end of the fiscal year).

Emergency services have to respond to major seasonal variations in needs and response capabilities. Vehicle transport on the Island during the summer, especially on weekends, is very difficult or impossible due to crowds on the beach. Saltaire and Ocean Beach have both attempted to create emergency access

---

[29] The following communities and villages have volunteer fire departments: Kismet, Saltaire, Fair Harbor, Ocean Beach, Ocean Bay Park, Cherry Grove, Fire Island Pines, and Davis Park.

lanes on the beach, but these lanes are met with public opposition and have not always been effective. Additionally, emergency medical incidents have a much higher frequency in summer months; for example, Ocean Beach had 300 medical calls in the summer of 2009. The Fair Harbor and Saltaire Fire districts combined had 150 drivable rescues in the 2009 summer season, about half of which were trauma patients. When the bay ices over in the winter, emergency services on the eastern end of the Island become extremely limited. Also, eastern communities have little or no emergency personnel or volunteer responders present during parts of the winter season; occasionally fires have gone undetected for hours or days before emergency personnel from Long Island or from western communities were notified.

School District

The Fire Island School District transports 61 students and 20 teachers and staff five days a week during the school year, which runs from September through June (not concurrent with the heaviest period of seasonal visitation). The daily transport of 81 people over five miles of "roadless" barrier island and to various destinations on Long Island is dictated by a logistically-complex transportation system.

The School District transportation system is designed to get students and staff to school as safely and efficiently as possible. The system is also structured to support a high quality of education for students, including multiple bus routes to allow students to participate in extracurricular activities. School Board members are sensitive to the cost efficiency of the transportation system, as transportation costs represent the second largest budget item for the School District (after staffing), costing up to $500,000 per year. School Board members regularly review bus routes and schedules to ensure efficiencies, recognizing that additional opportunities for efficiency could result in cost-savings. In general, Fire Island residents seem supportive of the school bus system.

The School District owns seven school buses, all of which are four-wheel drive and designed to operate over both paved and soft sand routes. A summary of the 27 routes that make up the Fire Island School District transportation system can be found in Appendix C. The buses also provide transportation for afterschool activities at the Woodhull School, as applicable, and occasionally transport parents and students to evening school events.

NPS Rangers and Staff

Like other user groups on Fire Island, NPS rangers, resource management, and maintenance staff utilize a mix of water- and vehicle-based travel modes to get around the Island. While boats are the primary method of cross-bay travel during the summer season, park staff also need vehicles to patrol on the Island. They use trucks or four-wheel-drive UTVs, stored on the Island at NPS sites, to travel to or between work sites. Their Polaris UTVs can carry up to two people as well as some equipment (including medical equipment). NPS owns golf carts for medical use and to transport handicapped persons. The park also has a four-wheel-drive front-end loader with forks on it. Additionally, NPS rents a horse for patrol in the eastern part of the Island, including the Otis Pike Wilderness. The horse is considered to have more advantages in public relations than transportation efficiency, as horses are not a cost-effective way to do business.

NPS maintains three shops at Talisman, Watch Hill, and Sailors Haven, used for the storage of tools and materials. The caching concept generally works for the rangers, allowing them to make fewer trips off the Island. However, the system is highly contingent upon strong communication and planning to replace supplies and keep the shops in order. Rangers are reluctant to leave building materials on the Island because of security concerns. Many of these storage supply areas and other NPS buildings are closed in the winter, which is one reason that rangers drive more during these months; they need greater mobility to access supplies. Other reasons cited for heavier use of vehicles during the winter include the comfort and safety of vehicles over boats in cold weather and the time and expense involved in winterizing boats or removing them before storms.

Although the rangers often work in similar areas of the Island and share equipment and storage sites, travel patterns differ by ranger division. Several of these divisional differences present challenges for travel coordination. For example, the law enforcement division needs their own vehicles and boats to respond to emergencies, which are unpredictable. Many resource management rangers live at Watch Hill and their travel needs differ from employees based on Long Island. The maintenance division works an earlier shift to complete jobs before the crowds arrive, while the wildlife division sets hours depending on the birds. The interpretive division, whose rangers operate according to a predetermined schedule, can rely less on vehicles and are able to coordinate more with others to meet their travel needs. Occasionally they will use a Polaris to move rangers laterally. Most rangers note that there is the potential for greater travel coordination, but doing so would require a significant time investment and more flexibility on the part of all rangers.

Even with the many divisions operating independently, NPS rangers as a whole believe that the number of vehicles in their fleet is sufficient to meet ranger needs. However, the harsh driving conditions on the Island lead to accelerated deterioration of vehicles. Rangers note a beach vehicle has a life of only 35,000 to 40,000 miles and that updated or more reliable vehicles would be helpful.

Residents

Residential travel patterns were not studied in-depth for this report, but a few general trends emerged. In the Ethnographic Overview and Assessment, researchers noted that nearly all Fire Island residents interviewed highly valued the peacefulness and laid-back atmosphere, which they related to the "roadless" nature of the Island. The absence of vehicles was an important draw for year-round and seasonal residents alike, contributing to the uniqueness of the place that made the expense and travel worthwhile. On the other hand, there is a sense among workers and year-round residents on the Island that driving regulations are the result of complaints by seasonal residents.

Current driving regulations allow 145 driving permits to be distributed to year-round residents, with only one vehicle permitted per household (at the time of publication, there were 141 driving permits in use by year-round residents). A few households have more than one vehicle permit due to municipal employees or contractors who are also year-round residents. Part-time residents who held a residential driving permits as of January 1, 1978, are permitted to maintain these permits, but no new permits are being issued and permits can only be inherited by spouses or life partners upon the death of the permit holder. The goal of the NPS is to eventually reduce part-time permits to zero.

Seasonal residents are generally not driving on Fire Island, as their permits are extremely limited and their period of residence often does not overlap with the residential driving season (Appendix B contains the 2010 driving dates for all user groups). Year-round residents, on the other hand, do rely on their vehicles, particularly during the winter as ferry service diminishes or stops completely. Anecdotal evidence gathered from interviews with on-Island residents and NPS staff suggests that residents tend to travel mostly to Long Island for work, errands, or personal events rather than using their vehicles to travel between communities. Residents who own vehicles tend to store them on Fire Island. Currently the NPS does not require permits UTVs and golf carts, as these generally operate within communities and not on Federal lands.

Conclusions / Observations

All people who live, work, or recreate on Fire Island rely on driving in some way to make their experience possible. From the water mains repaired by truck to the vehicle delivery of specialty landscaping materials, driving is an integral part of the many large and small operations on Fire Island. Yet despite the importance of vehicles to the Fire Island transportation system, most user groups make special efforts to minimize their driving footprint, either by regulation or by choice. Residents, employees, and visitors understand that driving must occur in balance with the protection of the Island's natural and cultural resources. In general, this balance is preserved and driving occurs only as needed to complement the water-based travel modes.

However, conflicts over driving do occur between user groups, and the long history of negotiation over driving relations has led to sensitivities on this topic among many Island stakeholders. The feasibility of choosing water-based transport instead of driving is subjective and varies by user group, by season, and by section of the Island. Many user groups call for greater flexibility and common sense when it comes to driving, noting that blanket policies cannot adequately apply to all sections of the Island and all times of the year.

Understanding the complex motivations and needs behind driving on Fire Island can help guide future management decisions. Infrastructure investments and policy changes aimed to increase water-based transportation, as called for in the Seashore's guidance documents, must be sensitive to the current patterns of vehicular transportation and the ways in which these patterns are integral to certain functions of Island life. The descriptions of vehicular patterns contained in this section are important tools for NPS and community managers to inform decisions about future transportation policy on Fire Island.

Section 6: Conclusions

The nature of Fire Island changes drastically on a seasonal basis, from a desolate and sparsely populated place in the off-season, to a bustling park and resort with over 20,000 people moving about on any given summer day. Fire Island hosts competing interests, including a spectrum of residents and visitors as well as workers and rangers who keep the Island operational for human enjoyment and for the preservation of its unique natural resources.

Findings and Trends

The Existing Conditions Report is primarily a review of the daily operations of life and travel on Fire Island. In the course of describing such operations, several important findings emerge:

- First, the Fire Island transportation system has evolved over a long period of time, in response to a complexity of factors including physical and political geography, the external (regional) transportation system, the extreme seasonality of residency and use on the Island, the environmental preservation mission of the National Seashore, and very significant infrastructure constraints in the face of heavy and diverse transportation needs and uses. As FIIS conducts the process of revising its GMP, the examination of expanded water transportation use is concurrent with calls for greater flexibility in the regulations on driving.

    In many ways, the current system offers the most efficient transportation for its users, who all face their own constraints (e.g., monetary, geographic, seasonal, safety-related, etc.) and NPS may have difficulty changing established travel patterns. As one stakeholder expressed, one small change to a transportation system on the Island can have very large and unpredictable consequences. Unsurprisingly, priorities differ among Island user groups, and transportation policies based on one group's priorities may be insensitive or unacceptable to another user group.

    It may be necessary to change some of the underlying conditions in order to identify and realize opportunities to improve transportation. Expansion of marine transport may well require significant changes elsewhere, as in shoreside and inland infrastructure, political negotiation and agreements on cooperative use, even a new generation of "green," quiet vehicles to reduce negative impacts on people's lives.

- Second, the system is currently a fairly successful intermodal network, including diverse terrestrial modes, both to Fire Island's gateways and on the Island itself. The NPS's emphasis on expanded use of water-based transportation must recognize that the origins and destinations of most people and goods coming to Fire Island are not docks or other waterfront locales. Terrestrial transport modes are necessary linkages to bring people and goods to docks and arinas, and these modes must be operational on infrastructure that is often not conducive to vehicles.

- There are many impediments, real and perceived, that block coordination and consolidation of travel solutions, sometimes within one user group or agency. For example, the multiple departments of LIPA and Verizon each maintain their own vehicles, and even the National Park Service ranger divisions are unable to make cross-bay trips simultaneously. It should be recognized that the constraints working against such collaborative travel scheduling are significant, yet these may also represent opportunity areas for greater system efficiencies.

Section 7: Opportunities

This transportation analysis is based upon the following General Management Plan (GMP) planning alternative: "Recognizing the Relationship between Humans and Nature." We anticipate, however, that the transportation opportunities identified herein will have relevance for each of the four GMP alternatives. The National Park Service (NPS) requested that we examine vehicle use on Fire Island, to better inform vehicle use and to look for opportunities to improve or expand water transport and enhance the roadless character of Fire Island. We note that many of the conflicts and sensitivities related to driving regulations, as described in the Existing Conditions section, had been recently expressed through the Negotiated Rulemaking process, and the definition of specific problems for the purposes of this transportation analysis may have conflicted with the conclusions of the Negotiated Rulemaking. Recognizing the sensitivity of this topic, these opportunities nonetheless include some that may be less amenable to some stakeholder groups and require strong partnership building efforts.

The opportunities focus on vehicle use reduction and enhanced use of water transportation, as well as ideas aimed at general improvement of the efficiency and function of the whole transportation system on and around Fire Island. In following the organization of the Existing Conditions report, these opportunities have been organized mainly by transportation service, as well as one particular mode (bicycles), and each includes the following components:

- *Possible Long-Term Outcomes:* This is a vision of an outcome or situation that NPS may want to achieve at least 10 years from now, and work towards in the interim.

- *Considerations:* These are existing constraints and opportunities relevant to this policy outcome.

- *Strategies:* These are concrete actions that can be taken within the next five years to work towards the identified outcome. NPS will likely not pursue all of these strategies but rather adopt strategies selectively, based on needs and priorities.

General

- Possible Long-Term Outcomes
    - NPS and Fire Island communities have a set of shared goals that govern the planning and operations of transportation systems on Fire Island. These goals respond to a clearly defined transportation problem that considers the needs of diverse user groups and the unique situation of life on Fire Island.
    - Both seasonal and year-round residents have a solid understanding of how transportation systems on Fire Island work, including the constraints and challenges of living on a roadless barrier island. They have established their communities and lifestyles to limit unnecessary travel and to accept the added transportation costs that come with living on Fire Island. While they try to minimize the negative externalities of vehicular transportation, such as noise, aesthetic, and safety impacts, to serve the basic needs of residents and visitors, residents also understand the necessity of such transportation and tolerate the impacts.
- Considerations
    - Various user groups expressed strong opinions about transportation on Fire Island, due in part to perceived threats to the status quo for various user groups. However, the specific transportation elements or impacts that are considered problematic often go undefined, which makes it difficult to address any problem in a way that really mitigates its negative impact.
    - Conflicts between user groups often result from misunderstandings about the needs and priorities of each group. Most user groups have structured their activities to operate within transportation systems specifically designed to accommodate the roadless character of the island. The details of the operations of these transportation systems may not be widely understood by the public or by other user groups. Several stakeholders suggest that a greater level of understanding among all user groups on Fire Island may alleviate perceived transportation issues.
- Strategies
    - Produce a "Best Practices Report" that describes community or user group practices that are well-aligned with Fire Island National Seashore's goals and mission (such as hauling garbage by water, providing dock space for utilities, and doing construction projects by barge instead of bringing equipment by vehicle). Such a report could serve as a model for other communities and user groups, who may be seeking proven and cost-effective means to reduce vehicle use. NPS may also identify incentives or recognition for communities that adopt best practices or establish long-term park goals to make these best practices more widespread.
    - Produce a "Fire Island Transportation User's Manual" or "Driver's Manual" to educate residents, workers, and visitors about transportation systems on Fire Island. This would explain costs associated with freight, garbage collection, and other services. It could also establish best practices for residents and workers to enhance water-based transportation and limit driving, in conjunction with the NPS's mission.

Coordination
- Possible Long-Term Outcomes
    - Agencies and businesses conducting work on Fire Island employ a well-coordinated transportation system founded on detailed communications between departments, divisions, and employees. Agencies and businesses coordinate services such as cross-bay trips to Fire Island, lateral movement along Fire Island, emergency or last-minute transport to Fire Island, storage of materials on Fire Island, and employee shifts and commuting. Such coordination saves time and money for all involved.
    - Cross-bay ferry trips are coordinated to offer service during key commuting times for Fire Island workers, particularly during weekdays and shoulder seasons. Timing has been coordinated with a group of Island workers (including NPS staff, contractors, utilities, and essential service personnel), who make adjustments as feasible to their work schedules to better utilize ferry services.
    - A cooperative climate exists between groups working on Fire Island (including NPS staff, contractors, utilities, and essential service personnel) such that individuals or small groups maintain frequent communication and may share boats or on-island vehicles for cross-bay and lateral transportation. Groups have established systems of compensation or cooperative agreements for the sharing of these resources.
    - NPS serves as a model for other user groups by having a highly-coordinated transportation system in which different divisions share resources, vehicles, boats, and storage areas. A transportation team, consisting of representatives from each division, meets and communicates regularly to identify new opportunities to synchronize travel while respecting the unique needs and schedules of the various NPS divisions.
- Considerations
    - Currently, ferry services generally operate at times that will run a profit, but many workers note that they cannot use the ferries for commuting during the off-season because ferry schedules do not correspond with work schedules. (One exception is Fire Island Ferry, which runs a morning and afternoon ferry to serve on-island workers from mid-March through mid-December.) Coordination will likely require compromises or negotiation on behalf of both workers and ferry operators, including the possibility of using smaller boats at these times (e.g., those currently used for water taxi service). However, ferries will strive to operate at maximum profitability.
    - The cross-bay ferry companies mainly serve the summer seasonal population (especially considering measures of patronage and revenue). Like the lateral ferry service provider, the cross-bay companies are responsive to the needs of this market, and current levels of service are sufficient to meet demand. Moreover, any such opportunities for improvement would not appreciably affect driving on Fire Island since driving regulations are most restrictive during summer months. Given that ferry companies are operating for profitability and will add trips that turn a profit, the only way to increase service during shoulder seasons or winter months would be to coordinate closely with potential users to ensure a critical mass of ridership or goods.
    - Many user groups noted that, even within a single agency or company, different departments had different transportation needs and schedules. There appears to be a significant opportunity for coordination within companies or agencies, in addition to long-term opportunities among companies/agencies.

- o NPS does make efforts to coordinate travel, especially cross-bay trips, and to use ferry service for seasonal employees. However, most divisions have different schedules or different equipment needs, cited as reasons for limited coordination. There appear to be opportunities to strengthen coordination through improved planning, though doing so would require a greater time investment on the part of NPS staff.
- Strategies
  - o Actively seek out opportunities to coordinate travel between NPS divisions. This could be institutionally encouraged by offering incentives such as technical assistance for shared travel or new communication strategies that result in greater transportation consolidation. NPS may also add a specific objective to future management plans to better coordinate travel, add travel coordination as an agenda item for park leadership or interdepartmental meetings, and/or shift work schedules (as feasible) to accommodate shared travel. Areas where NPS is successful at travel coordination can be promoted and marketed among other user groups that have similar travel needs and constraints.
  - o NPS could facilitate a meeting between ferry operators and on-island workers to discuss potential for coordinating service. One outcome of this meeting could be a pilot project to increase commuter service during the shoulder season, in which the ferry companies agree to provide additional service and the workers agree to maintain a certain level of ridership during the defined pilot period. Results from such a pilot can be studied to see what opportunities and constraints exist to increased off-season ferry service.
  - o NPS could offer incentives for utilities, essential services, and contractors that coordinate travel and/or increase use of water-based transport. This would require the collection of baseline data for current levels of coordination and water-based transport and a means to document coordination. Incentives could include reduced permit fees or space for storage facilities on NPS lands.

Vehicles
- Long-term outcomes/policies goals
    - Vehicles that operate on Fire Island are encouraged to reduce noise and pollution, such as through the use of battery-powered and alternative fuel propulsion. NPS pilots the use of alternative fuel vehicles, based on best practices elsewhere in the Park Service and in accordance with the Climate Friendly Parks Initiative; this can serve as a model for other user groups on Fire Island.
    - All drivers are permitted and follow all driving regulations, which are enforced cooperatively by NPS rangers and other law enforcement partners. Island residents and visitors understand that vehicles are operating legally and fulfilling a specific purpose.
- Considerations
    - Summer visitors and seasonal residents are not a significant constituent of drivers on Fire Island. Visitor surveys show, and NPS license data confirm, that most driving is by year-round residents and service providers on Fire Island. The summer season includes peaks of permitted driving activity by police and emergency services and significant driving activity by utility service providers. It may also be the peak of activity for other vehicles such as golf carts, four-wheelers, and other small utility vehicles used for carrying goods to residences and businesses. There are no data characterizing these small vehicles.
    - Shoulder seasons are clearly the peak times for permitted driving activity, including contractor vehicles and school buses, neither of which run in the summer. There is also evidence that these seasons are becoming more popular with retired people and other visitor groups. It is possible, therefore, that this confluence has increased complaints about vehicle use.
    - Widespread use of battery-powered vehicles would require charging stations around Fire Island. NPS may consider providing this infrastructure in the future as a means of encouraging the use of these vehicles.
    - There are some complaints about enforcement of driving regulations, including anecdotal evidence that the checkpoints are not strictly monitored and that NPS Rangers do not have the staff capacity to enforce regulations 24 hours a day. NPS staff has asked that the Suffolk County Marine Bureau help enforce regulations.
    - Vehicle use in general and driving regulations in particular are highly sensitive topics among all Fire Island vehicle user groups, in part because their operations have been affected by the recently-concluded Negotiated Rulemaking process, impending new regulations, and by other regulations restricting driving promulgated by NPS. Strategies in this area may best be pursued on a long-range time scale, including outreach and consensus-building activities.
- Strategies
    - Explore incentives to reduce noise and emissions (such as fee reductions for battery-powered vehicles or other low-emission vehicles, fee supplements for higher-emitting or high-noise vehicles).
    - Conduct a resident/visitor survey or public workshop to identify the aspects of on-island vehicle use that are most problematic (noise, sight, emissions, energy use, roads, etc.). Use this information to target specific solutions that allow essential vehicle use to continue but mitigate the most offensive impacts.

- Monitor the type and frequency of use of small utility vehicles (UTVs), including seasonality and storage of these vehicles to fully characterize the vehicles and their potential future uses. Consider potential substitutions of UTVs for full-size service vehicles, and identify conflicts potentially arising with proliferation of UTV use. NPS might also consider permitting these vehicles, particularly those that cross into NPS lands, or partnering with towns and villages to further study UTV use.
- Consider the feasibility of improving certain road surfaces to better accommodate electric vehicles. This approach would require careful planning, monitoring and enforcement to ensure that improved road surfaces would not encourage more use of conventional vehicles.
- Monitor vehicle use on Fire Island to include counts of vehicles used during certain days/times/seasons to better quantify volumes of vehicle traffic and purposes of use. Data would be used to identify future opportunities to reduce vehicle traffic.

Freight
- Possible Long-Term Outcomes
    - Garbage and debris are generally transported off of Fire Island by boat, which is an efficient and cost-effective means of disposal. Most communities have docks that are capable of garbage hauling, and those that do not pay a fee to have their garbage hauled by land to a neighboring dock. A fleet of UTVs based on Fire Island helps to deliver garbage and debris to collection points, and these vehicles are stored unobtrusively throughout the communities and NPS lands. We note it may be impractical to haul some types of debris off-Island by boat; however, the general idea is to maximize boat haulage and minimize vehicle use and negative effects (noise, emissions, etc.).
    - Freight movement is streamlined such that freight can go by barge year-round (weather permitting) and can efficiently accommodate special requests, last-minute jobs, and construction materials. The significant shift in water-based freight is driven by stronger coordination on the part of customers, who understand and expect that freight works around a structured schedule.
- Considerations
    - Garbage haulage from Corneille Estates and all communities to the west is by vehicle, via the NPS gate and Robert Moses State Park, while six of the ten communities have docks with freight capability (see Figures 7 and 8 for freight capabilities).
    - Many communities do not currently have docks that can handle garbage hauling. Communities with those capabilities have expressed hesitance to serve as transfer points for other communities' garbage.
    - There are some mismatches between dock capabilities and land-based infrastructure, e.g., Saltaire's renovated dock has capacity for vehicles and other heavy equipment but walks in the Village that cannot accommodate the equipment. This is due to limited funding and capacity for capital improvements and long-range planning.
    - Contractors often drive empty trucks onto the Island (since freight is carted over by ferry) and then drive off the Island with construction debris. They say that it is unfeasible to transfer debris by boat, especially since trucks are needed at both sides of the transfer.
    - Anecdotally, cost seems to be the biggest barrier to water-based hauling.
    - Smaller, less obtrusive vehicles could be used to haul garbage to docks (as is now done in Ocean Beach), but these vehicles would need to be stored within communities.
    - Vehicle-based garbage hauling is already constrained by seasonal driving restrictions, tides, and beach closures for piping plovers. The result is large garbage trucks driving through communities at very early hours.
    - Certain items cannot feasibly (or easily) be moved by boat (sand, stone, certain fragile materials, some kinds of debris).
- Strategies
    - Evaluate the actual cost differentials between water-based hauling and vehicle-based hauling. Present findings in a form that is accessible to Island seasonal and year-round residents to facilitate a public forum on the value of water-based hauling.
    - Explore fee structures that would allow communities to share existing freight docks (e.g., increasing users' hauling fees in communities without freight docks and decreasing users' fees in communities with freight docks). Conduct a survey of community leaders and residents to determine the feasibility of such a cooperative arrangement.

- Identify sites on Fire Island (in communities and on NPS lands) that could be used to store UTV garbage hauling vehicles. Identify a fee structure that would allow communities that store such vehicles to have reduced hauling fees.
- Examine opportunities to improve roads, operations, and scheduling (within very specific, known, and short windows when haulers would move between communities) to allow inter-village haulage and achieve net overall reductions of [smaller] vehicle use.
- Create a "Fire Island Transportation User's Manual" that includes a section on freight schedules, capabilities, and constraints. The goal is for Fire Island residents to understand that transfer of certain types of materials/goods has associated costs and time requirements, and this should be accepted as part of island life.

Lateral Transport
- Possible Long-Term Outcomes
  - Utilities, contractors, essential services, and other on-island workers use a mix of privately-owned boats, public ferry services, and private vehicles to move laterally along Fire Island, with most transport taking place by water and supplemented by smaller vehicles to move materials within communities.
  - A more robust water-taxi system is supported by workers on weekdays and during shoulder season, and by residents and visitors during weekends and the summer season. The taxi service is able to offer more frequent and reliable service because more people use the system.
- Considerations
  - The current, limited lateral water taxi service has its service and revenue focus on the summer market; we would defer the identification of new summer market opportunities to the service provider, with the argument that enhancing this service would not reduce vehicle use on the Island. However, the water taxi runs in the same direction – lateral – as do many of Fire Island's service vehicles, and it is possible that some mode substitution could occur with the right service, accommodation and cost structure.
  - Several users have heavy vehicular lateral traffic that may be substituted (all or in part) by water-based transport:
    - Suffolk County Water Administration (SCWA): Three Polarises (UTVs) used for daily maintenance at pump stations (chemical treatment and sample collection) located in most communities. In summer/shoulder seasons, operators could potentially use ferry service to access Fire Island and an SCWA boat to move between the communities. Operators would deliver service to individual pumps on foot with chemicals and supplies moved by hand carts already stored near community docks. This also may require storage of Polarises in a few communities for larger jobs with heavier equipment.
    - Verizon: Provides 24-hour emergency response by vehicles onto and around the island. Work by the Verizon construction department requires heavy equipment (4-wheel-drive vehicles). There does not appear to be a solid opportunity for a marine mode switch.
    - Long Island Power Administration (LIPA): Much of LIPA's work also requires heavy equipment, but some work (like meter reading) does not. Interviews indicated that employees try to maximize ferry use and that LIPA now uses a small craft (and a bicycle) for some lateral island movement. LIPA may have an opportunity to expand on the small craft approach, especially for meter readers during summer and shoulder seasons.
  - Many private employers cited lack of dock space as one of the key reasons they use vehicles instead of boats. Boats would be faster in many cases. However, community docks generally do not maintain slips for these workers, especially during peak summer months, due to heavy demand for use of slips by residents and visitors. The current storage situation for privately-owned work boats includes:
    - LIPA maintains a slip for their boat in Ocean Beach, and they have not had problems with temporary docking in other communities for short jobs.
    - SCPD stores their boats on Long Island.

- Users employing water taxi services or private boats for lateral transportation may need storage spaces in communities.
- Strategies
    - Create a pilot program for lateral water taxi service to run on a regular schedule during the shoulder season (developed in cooperation with a group or groups of workers, who would use the service during the pilot).
    - Conduct a study that documents formal constraints and barriers to workers using private boats for lateral travel (including opportunities and barriers for shared dock space).
    - Encourage communities to include a small number of slips at their docks for use of Fire Island workers (especially utilities and essential services). This could be a goal to add to their long-term community or village plans. This could be done through disseminating the benefits of water-based utility and essential services work and resulting reduction of vehicle traffic in the community.

Bicycles
- Possible Long-Term Outcomes
    - Bicycles are a safe, feasible means of lateral transport in the western communities, for workers traveling to job sites and for residents traveling around Fire Island (not intended for visitor recreational purposes). Bicycling will be accommodated by links to and amenities within other transportation modes and physical infrastructure.
- Considerations
    - There are physical constraints that limit the feasibility of bicycle use, including lack of transport of bicycles by ferries, congested walks during summer months that would be unsafe for cyclists, and lack of bicycle access over the Robert Moses Causeway.
    - The Town of Brookhaven prohibits bicycle use on boardwalks, which effectively prohibits bicycle use community-wide in Cherry Grove, Fire Island Pines, Water Island and Davis Park, where the only pathways are boardwalks or soft sand.
    - NPS prohibits bicycle use on park boardwalks.
    - If bicycles are to be used for lateral transportation, communities will need to work together to provide seamless connections across community borders.
    - Many Fire Island residents and visitors strongly oppose a separated or paved bike path along portions of Burma Road at this time. If such a path were to be built in the future, in conjunction with changing circumstances and opinions, it could only be done after significant study and cooperation among Fire Island stakeholders.
- Strategies
    - Communities, ferry operators, and NPS will need to work collectively to set goals for the type of transportation-related bicycle use to be accommodated (including setting certain dates or times of day for bicycle use, determining what types of user groups should be prioritized, etc.).
    - Pilot lateral bicycle routes by designating walks or routes between communities as "bike routes." A pilot program should be limited to the shoulder season, weekdays only, and established in conjunction with Fire Island employees who can use and provide feedback on the route. These routes will be targeted towards employees and residents, not intended for visitor recreation.
    - Establish an inter-community Bicycle Working Group to identify specific benefits and impacts of expanding bicycles as a lateral transportation option. The Working Group would include representatives from communities, ferry operators, and NPS to set goals for the type of bicycle use to be accommodated (including setting certain dates or times of day for bicycle use, determining what types of user groups should be prioritized, etc.). The Working Group would produce recommendations on how to best accommodate transportation-relating cycling and what level of bicycling would be feasible on Fire Island.
    - Explore the feasibility of a removable surface to lie over certain sections of the Burma Road to accommodate transportation-related cycling on a seasonal basis, for example, during summer and on shoulder season weekends or during shoulder-season weekdays for workers.

Appendix A: Stakeholder Table

Source: Volpe Center

Stakeholder Group	Needs and Interests	Strategy for Contact	Contact Information
Contractors	<ul><li>80 contractors have permits; 22 are on the waiting list for driving permits.</li><li>Busiest season for contractors is April 1 through Memorial Day (driving season is October – May), but work goes on year-round.</li><li>Contractors that work in eastern communities generally have their own boats; boats are quicker than driving for communities east of Atlantique.</li><li>Contractors are provided with reduced rate tickets, free parking with Fire Island Ferries (October through March).</li><li>Usually contractors still elect to drive for convenience; business models built around driving.<ul><li>History of conflict with NPS over driving regulations.</li></ul></li><li>Contractors induce demand for ferry service (often travel the opposite direction as residents and help supplement service for residents; contractor driving hurts ferry service.</li></ul>	<ul><li>Jay Lippert and Diane Abell identified and invited contractors to participate in stakeholder meeting (December 3, 2009).</li><li>All contractors present at meeting were year-round FIIS residents.</li></ul>	Walter Boss - 631-597-6262 (Waltboss@earthlink.net) Kevin Burke - 631-583-5581 (kmsgburke@optonline.net) Forrest Clark - 516-524-9999 (fpclark@yahoo.com) Joseph Loeffler - 631-583-5940 (jay.sea@verizon.net) James Ragusa – 631-583-5995 (Ragusamy@msn.com) Brendan Reynolds – 631-379-1482 (rklandrt@aol.com) Barry Wetherall - 631-581-0993
Emergency services	<ul><li>Includes police, fire, and emergency medical care.</li><li>Primary concerns are moving people as quickly and safely as possible and getting manpower and equipment to the location of the incident.</li><li>Combination of community, village, town, county, and Federal services.</li><li>Most incidents occur in summer, when beach driving is dangerous/unfeasible.</li><li>Need for emergency vehicle access route along the beach.</li><li>Emergency services provided only by certain communities with lots of mutual aid.</li></ul>	<ul><li>Project team made phone calls to fire and police personnel from Villages, Towns, and County</li><li>Jay Lippert convened a stakeholder group from the Law Enforcement Council on December 3, 2009. The meeting included representatives from the Towns of Islip and Brookhaven, the Village of Saltaire, and Suffolk County.</li></ul>	P.O. Bob Cappadona - 631-854-8382 Salvatore Garafalo - 631-451-6262 (sgarafalo@brookhaven.org) Rick Gimbl - 631-224-5730 (rgimbl@townofislip-ny.gov) Vernon Henriksen - 631-793-4366 (vhmasel@aol.com) Lou Pouletsos - 631-451-6262 (lpouletsos@brookhaven.org) Lt. Ken Sandtory - 631-854-8382 (kentory@aol.com)
Utilities	<ul><li>3 utility companies have fleet driving permits.</li><li>Utilities are defined as water, electric, gas delivery, and phone companies.</li><li>Some utilities leave their vehicles on the beach or in towns (including Verizon and Suffolk County Water Authority).<ul><li>Desirable to minimize trips.</li><li>Potential to create a secure parking area to leave vehicles.</li></ul></li><li>Within a single utility, different divisions have different transportation needs and operate separate fleets/vehicles.</li><li>Challenges of working within large corporations to meet Island-specific needs and of permit acquisition.</li></ul>	<ul><li>Diane Abell invited a Suffolk County Water representative to attend a stakeholder meeting on December 4, 2009.</li><li>NPS provided initial contacts for Verizon and LIPA/National Grid. Phone interviews were conducted in late December 2009 and early January 2010.</li></ul>	Paul Kuzman, Suffolk County Water Authority - 631-563-0339 (pkuzman@scwa.com) Jim Memola, Long Island Power Authority - 631-348-6128 (james.memola@us.ngrid.com) Tom Powers, Verizon - 631-491-9966 (thomas.j.powers@verizon.com) Ralph Porco, Verizon (ralph.v.porco.jr@verizon.com) Jen Higgins, Verizon Dave Lucas, Verizon
Ferry operators and concessioners	<ul><li>Interested in maximizing profits while meeting operational regulations; schedules are based on demand for service.</li><li>Davis Park and Sayville Ferry operate as concessioners to NPS for Watch Hill and Sailors Haven service.</li></ul>	<ul><li>NPS staff arranged a meeting on September 18, 2009, with Fire Island Ferry, and a second meeting on December 3, 2009, with Sayville</li></ul>	Dave Anderson, Fire Island Ferries - 631-665-3600 Luke Kaufman, Fire Island Ferries - 631-665-3600

Category	Notes	Contacts
(Ferries, cont.)	• Observations of declining ridership among certain markets. • Fleets must be capable of very high seasonal ridership and lower off-season ridership and accommodate variable weather conditions. • Concessions employ approximately 80 to 100 employees, some of whom live at Watch Hill; most travel by ferry and must coordinate with DP Ferry. • Some problems with storage of building materials and timing of ferries to accommodate restaurant at Watch Hill.	Ken Stein, Sayville Ferry - 631-589-0810 Charles Sherman, Davis Park Ferry - 631-475-1665 Matthew Sherman, Davis Park Ferry - 631-475-1665 Point O' Woods Ferry - 631-665-1568 Ferry and Davis Park Ferry. • The project team conducted additional phone and internet research for information about private ferry companies.
Municipal services	• Road and boardwalk maintenance is conducted seasonally by incorporated villages or by Islip and Brookhaven. • Within one town or village, different departments are responsible for maintenance of parks, walks, and other services. Often each department has its own fleet of vehicles or transportation patterns. • Villages can take advantage of on-Island storage and parking, whereas Towns must make multiple trips. • Communities often reluctant to share facilities (including docks and walks). • Many municipal employees use ferries during summer season; some key personnel are provided housing on-Island and others drive during off-season.	• NPS identified and invited municipal employees to participate in stakeholder meeting (December 4, 2009). Representatives from Ocean Beach, Saltaire, and Islip attended; Brookhaven did not send a representative but a Highway Department representative was interviewed by phone. George Hafele, Islip (ghafele@townofislip-ny.gov) Mario Posillico, Saltaire - 631-583-5566 (mario@saltaire.org) Kevin Schelling, Ocean Beach - 631-445-4589 William Stenger, Islip – (wstenger@townofislip-ny.gov) Ed Keiffert, Brookhaven – 631-451-9236

NPS staff	• Includes full-time, part-time, and volunteers (including those at Fire Island Lighthouse).
	• Ranger divisions include Interpretive, Law Enforcement, Maintenance, Resource Management, and Wildlife.
	• Ranger divisions operate separately based on their various duties and equipment but try to coordinate travel as feasible. Many divisions express the need to be independently mobile.
	• NPS owns a fleet of 22 boats, 20 Seashore-owned vehicles, seven GSA-owned vehicles, and 25 UTVs. Some are specific to a division and others are shared.
	   ○ Number of boats is sufficient.
	   ○ Number of vehicles is sufficient but vehicles could be more updated or reliable.
	• Rangers are responsible for enforcement of driving and resource regulations.
	• Ferry schedules are not consistent with the working schedule of most rangers, including rangers who live on-Island.
		• Jay Lippert convened a group of 11 rangers, representing all of the divisions, to attend a meeting on December 2, 2009.
		• The project team has maintained close contact with Jay Lippert and John Mahoney, Division of Visitor and Resource Protection.
		
		Michael Bilecki (michael_bilecki@nps.gov)
		Jim Dunphy (jim_dunphy@nps.gov)
		Jason Flynn (jason_flynn@nps.gov)
		Kaetlyn Kerr (Kaetlyn_kerr@nps.gov)
		Jay Lippert (jay_lippert@nps.gov)
		Walt Martens (walt_martens@nps.gov)
		Lindsay Ries (lindsay_ries@nps.gov)
		Irene Rosen (Irene_rosen@nps.gov)
		John Stewart (John_stewart@nps.gov)
		Jon Swindle (jon_swindle@nps.gov)
		Paula Valentine (paula_valentine@nps.gov)

School district	• Transport 61 students to five different schools (on and off Fire Island) every weekday during the school year. • Transport teachers and staff to the Woodhull School from Captree Island. • Maintain a fleet of seven school buses and eight drivers. • Priorities are safely getting students to school and ensuring they have opportunities for well-rounded education. • Constrained by state laws governing school transport.	• Jay Lippert, President of the Fire Island School Board, arranged a meeting with Loretta Ferraro, Superintendent of the Fire Island School District. Lori Ferraro - 631-583-5626 Jay Lippert - 631-687-4757

Essential Services	• Essential services consist of trash hauling, propane and gas delivery, plumbers, and electricians. A total of 30 permits are issued (mix of fleet and individual permits).
	• Daily vehicle movement for trash hauling.
	   ○ Use of larger vehicles for hauling trash off-Island in eastern communities.
	   ○ Use of smaller vehicles or UTVs for intra-community trash hauling.
	• Garbage haulers maintain separate systems for eastern and western communities, adaptable to dock infrastructure.
	• Challenge of needing frequent trash pick-up due, in part, to lack of storage facilities in communities.
		• NPS and Contractors provide background information on haulers and contacts for further research.
		
		Tommy Esposito, Tony's Barges – 631-589-2130

Appendix B: NPS 2010 Driving Dates & Times

Contractors & Business (includes plumbers and electricians)

- January 1-through April 30: Driving permitted in lieu of alternative transportation
- May 1 – May 21: Weekend Closures: Saturday and Sunday driving is not authorized. Driving permitted in lieu of alternative transportation during weekdays.
- **From Saturday May 22 through Monday October 11:** No driving.
- 3/15-Columbus Day Monday: No Smith Point Access in lieu of alternative transportation
- **From Tuesday October 12 through December 31:** Driving permitted in lieu of alternative transportation

Residents & Municipal

- January 1- through April 30: Driving permitted in lieu of alternative transportation.
- 3/15 through Labor Day: No Smith Point Access, east end drivers must enter through the West District Ranger Station.
- **From Saturday May 1 through May 23:** Weekend Restrictions: Weekend driving before 9am, and after 6 pm Saturdays & Sundays.
- **From May 28 (the Friday of Memorial Day) weekend through May 31 (Memorial Day):** No driving, 9 p.m. Friday through 6 p.m. Memorial Day Monday.
- **From June 1 through June 25 (the Last Friday in June)** Weekday Restrictions: Weekday driving only before 9 a.m. and after 6 p.m. <u>No weekend driving</u>
- **From June 26 (the last Saturday in June) through September 6 (Labor Day Monday):** No driving
- **From September 7 (the Tuesday after Labor Day) through September 10 (the Friday after Labor Day):** Weekday driving allowed. Driving before 9 a.m. and after 6 p.m.
- **From September 10 through September 12 (the first full weekend after Labor Day):** No Driving 9 p.m. Friday through 6 p.m. Sunday.
- **From September 13 (the 2nd Monday in September) through October 11:** Weekdays: Driving permitted in lieu of alternative transportation. Weekend Restrictions: Weekend driving before 9am, and after 6 pm Saturdays & Sundays, and Columbus Day Monday.
- **From October 12 through December 31:** Driving permitted in lieu of alternative transportation.

Essential Service: Fuel Providers and Carters

- January 1-through April 30: Driving permitted in lieu of alternative transportation.
- **From May 1 (the 1st Saturday of May) through May 27:** Weekday driving permitted. Weekend Restrictions: driving permitted before 9 a.m. and after 6 pm Saturdays & Sundays.
- **From May 28 (the Friday of Memorial Day weekend) through May 31 (Memorial Day):** No driving, 6 p.m. Friday through 6 p.m. Memorial Day Monday.
- **From June 01 through September 3 (the Friday before Labor Day):** Weekday driving permitted only before 9 a.m. and after 6 p.m. No weekend driving except for emergencies. No driving July 4 & Labor Day weekend.
- **From the September 7 through October 11:** Driving before 9am and after 6 pm Saturdays, Sundays, no driving Columbus Day Monday. Weekday driving allowed
- **From October 12 through December 31:** Driving permitted in lieu of alternative transportation
- 3/16 through October 11(Columbus Day Monday): No Smith Point access, east end drivers must enter through the West District Ranger Station.

Public Utility & Official

- **1/1 through May 21 (the Thursday before Memorial Day):** Driving permitted in lieu of alternative transportation.

- **From May 29 (Memorial Day Saturday) through September 06 (Labor Day Monday):** No weekend driving except for emergencies. No driving Memorial Day, July 4, & Labor Day weekends. Weekday driving permitted.
- **3/16 through Columbus Day Monday:** No Smith Point access, east end drivers must enter through the West District Ranger Station.
- **From September 7 (the Tuesday after Labor Day) through December 31:** Driving permitted in lieu of alternative transportation.

Appendix C: Fire Island School District Bus Routes

- **Route 1 (East Morning Run):** Picks up three students from Point O' Woods and Ocean Bay Park and drops them at Ocean Beach Fire House (for transport to secondary schools).
- **Route 2 (Islip High, Bay Shore High, Bay Shore Middle Morning Run):** Picks up nine students at Ocean Beach Fire House and four students from Robbins Rest and Atlantique and drops them at the Lonelyville hub.
- **Routes 3 and 4 (Islip High, Bay Shore High, Bay Shore Middle Morning Run):** One bus picks up nine students at Lonelyville hub and three students in other western communities and drops them off at Islip High and Bay Shore Middle. A second bus picks up seven students at Lonelyville hub and eight students in other western communities and drops them off at Bay Shore High.
- **Route 5 (Employee Morning Run, 6:30 a.m.):** Bus picks up five employees at the Captree parking lot and drops them off at the Woodhull School.
- **Route 6 (St. John the Baptist Morning Run):** Bus picks up two students on Fire Island and drives them to St. John the Baptist High.
- **Route 7 (St. Patrick's Morning Run):** Bus picks up three students on Fire Island and drives them to St. Patrick's School.
- **Route 8 (Employee Morning Run, 7 a.m.):** Bus picks up six employees at the Captree parking lot and two to three employees in western communities and drops them at The Woodhull School.
- **Route 9 (Employee Morning Run, 7:30 a.m.):** Bus picks up three to four employees at the Captree parking lot and five students at the Coast Guard Station and Kismet and drops them off at The Woodhull School.
- **Route 10 (West Beach Morning Run):** Bus picks up eighteen students from communities west of the Woodhull School and drops them at school.
- **Route 11 (East Beach Morning Run):** Bus picks up six students from communities east of the Woodhull School and drops them at school.
- **Route 12 (Employee Morning Run, 8:30 a.m.):** Bus picks up three employees from the Captree parking lot and drops them at the Woodhull School.
- **Route 13 (Pre-Kindergarten Dismissal West):** Bus picks up one student from the Woodhull School and drops her off at the Coast Guard Station.
- **Route 13A (Pre-Kindergarten Dismissal East):** Bus picks up two students from the Woodhull School and drops them off at eastern communities.
- **Route 14 (Employee 12 p.m. Run):** Bus brings one employee from the Woodhull School to the Captree parking lot.
- **Route 15 (Bay Shore High Dismissal):** Bus picks up 16 students at Bay Shore High and drops them in Fire Island communities.
- **Route 16 (Islip High Dismissal):** Bus picks up four students from Islip High and drops them in Fire Island communities.
- **Route 17 (Woodhull East Dismissal Run):** Bus brings three to four students from the Woodhull School to eastern communities.
- **Route 18 (Woodhull West Beach & Coast Guard):** Bus brings 21/22 students from the Woodhull School to western communities, the Coast Guard Station, and the YMCA Bay Shore.
- Routes 19-22 are employee, club, and library runs that are on-demand?
- **Route 23 (Bay Shore Middle Regular / Bay Shore High Late):** Bus picks up nine students from Bay Shore Middle plus Bay Shore High students that have called ahead to reserve and brings them to Fire Island communities
- **Route 24 (Private Schools Regular Dismissal Runs):** Bus picks up five students from St. Patrick's School and St. John the Baptist and brings them to Fire Island communities
- **Route 25-27 (Late Run Routes):** Bus picks up students from Long Island schools on a call-ahead basis.

	REPORT DOCUMENTATION PAGE		Form Approved OMB No. 0704-0188

The public reporting burden for this collection of information is estimated to average 1 hour per response, including the time for reviewing instructions, searching existing data sources, gathering and maintaining the data needed, and completing and reviewing the collection of information. Send comments regarding this burden estimate or any other aspect of this collection of information, including suggestions for reducing the burden, to Department of Defense, Washington Headquarters Services, Directorate for Information Operations and Reports (0704-0188), 1215 Jefferson Davis Highway, Suite 1204, Arlington, VA 22202-4302. Respondents should be aware that notwithstanding any other provision of law, no person shall be subject to any penalty for failing to comply with a collection of information if it does not display a currently valid OMB control number.
PLEASE DO NOT RETURN YOUR FORM TO THE ABOVE ADDRESS.

1. REPORT DATE (DD-MM-YYYY)	2. REPORT TYPE	3. DATES COVERED (From - To)
30-12-2011	Planning Report	September 2009 - May 2010

4. TITLE AND SUBTITLE	5a. CONTRACT NUMBER
Fire Island National Seashore Alternative Transportation Study	F4505087777
	5b. GRANT NUMBER
	5c. PROGRAM ELEMENT NUMBER

6. AUTHOR(S)	5d. PROJECT NUMBER
Dyer, Michael	PMIS 125892A/17089
Peckett, Haley	5e. TASK NUMBER
	NP63/NP64
	5f. WORK UNIT NUMBER

7. PERFORMING ORGANIZATION NAME(S) AND ADDRESS(ES)	8. PERFORMING ORGANIZATION REPORT NUMBER
U.S. Department of Transportation Research and Innovation Technology Administration John A. Volpe Transportation Systems Center 55 Broadway, Cambridge, MA 02142	DOT-VNTSC-NPS-12-01

9. SPONSORING/MONITORING AGENCY NAME(S) AND ADDRESS(ES)	10. SPONSOR/MONITOR'S ACRONYM(S)
U.S. Department of the Interior National Park Service Northeast Region 15 State Street, Boston, MA 02109	NPS NER & FIIS
	11. SPONSOR/MONITOR'S REPORT NUMBER(S)
	615/111458

12. DISTRIBUTION/AVAILABILITY STATEMENT
Public distribution/availability

13. SUPPLEMENTARY NOTES

14. ABSTRACT
As part of its General Management Plan (GMP) process, Fire Island National Seashore (FIIS) seeks to develop a long-term management model to protect Fire Island's resources, while facilitating a safe, rewarding, and relevant experience for the public. As part of this management model, the Seashore is seeking the best and most appropriate methods for moving people, goods, and services to, from, and along Fire Island. The transportation challenge addressed by this report is to balance the many kinds of vehicle use on the Island with the Seashore's resource protection mission and the desire of residents and visitors to preserve the Island's "roadless" nature. The existing conditions section characterize the diverse transportation systems currently in use on Fire Island, many of which have evolved to function in line with the island's roadless character. The opportunities section focuses on vehicle use reduction and enhanced use of water transportation, as well as ideas aimed at general improvement of the efficiency and function of the whole transportation system on and around Fire Island.

15. SUBJECT TERMS
national park, national seashore, park, alternative transportation, transportation, water-based transportation

16. SECURITY CLASSIFICATION OF:			17. LIMITATION OF ABSTRACT	18. NUMBER OF PAGES	19a. NAME OF RESPONSIBLE PERSON
a. REPORT	b. ABSTRACT	c. THIS PAGE			Peter Steele, NER, and Chris Soller, FIIS
None	None	None	NA	83	19b. TELEPHONE NUMBER (Include area code) 617-223-5130, NER/ 631-687-4751, FIIS

Standard Form 298 (Rev. 8/98)
Prescribed by ANSI Std. Z39.18

As the nation's principal conservation agency, the Department of the Interior has the responsibility for most of our nationally owned public lands and natural resources. This includes fostering sound use of our land and water resources; protecting our fish, wildlife, and biological diversity; preserving the environmental and cultural values of our parks and historic places; and providing for the enjoyment of life through outdoor recreation. The department assesses our energy and mineral resources and works to ensure that their development is in the best interests of all our people by encouraging stewardship and citizen participation in their care. The department also has a major responsibility for American Indian reservation communities and for people who live in island territories under U.S. administration.

615/111458/December 2011

www.ingramcontent.com/pod-product-compliance
Lightning Source LLC
Chambersburg PA
CBHW081842170526
45167CB00007B/2877